The *New* Daily Study Bible

The Letters of
John and Jude

The *New* Daily Study Bible

The Letters of
John and Jude

William Barclay

Westminster John Knox Press
LOUISVILLE • LONDON

© The William Barclay Estate, 1976, 2002

First edition published in 1958 as *The Daily Study Bible: The Letters of John and Jude*
Revised edition published in 1976
This third edition fully revised and updated by Saint Andrew Press and published as *The New Daily Study Bible: The Letters of John and Jude* in 2002

Published in the United States by
Westminster John Knox Press
Louisville, Kentucky

Cover design by McColl Productions Ltd, by courtesy of Saint Andrew Press

Typeset by Waverley Typesetters, Galashiels

PRINTED IN THE UNITED STATES OF AMERICA

02 03 04 05 06 07 08 09 10 11 — 10 9 8 7 6 5 4 3 2 1

Library of Congress Cataloging-in-Publication Data is on file at the Library of Congress, Washington, D.C.

ISBN 0-664-22557-8

To

MY FRIEND

P.M.S.

A GREAT ENCOURAGER

CONTENTS

1 JOHN

2 JOHN

3 JOHN

JOHN AND JUDE

JUDE

SERIES FOREWORD
(by Ronnie Barclay)

My father always had a great love for the English language
and its literature. As a student at the University of Glasgow,
he won a prize in the English class – and I have no doubt
that he could have become a Professor of English instead
of Divinity and Biblical Criticism. In a pre-computer age, he
had a mind like a computer that could store vast numbers of
quotations, illustrations, anecdotes and allusions; and, more
remarkably still, he could retrieve them at will. The editor of
this revision has, where necessary, corrected and attributed
the vast majority of these quotations with considerable skill
and has enhanced our pleasure as we read quotations from
Plato to T. S. Eliot.

There is another very welcome improvement in the new
text. My mother was one of five sisters, and my grandmother
was a commanding figure as the Presbyterian minister's
wife in a small village in Ayrshire in Scotland. She ran that
small community very efficiently, and I always felt that my
father, surrounded by so many women, was more than some-
what overawed by it all! I am sure that this is the reason why
his use of English tended to be dominated by the words 'man',
'men' and so on, with the result that it sounded very male-
orientated. Once again, the editor has very skilfully improved
my father's English and made the text much more readable
for all of us by amending the often one-sided language.

It is a well-known fact that William Barclay wrote at break-
neck speed and never corrected anything once it was on

paper – he took great pride in mentioning this at every possible opportunity! This revision, in removing repetition and correcting the inevitable errors that had slipped through, has produced a text free from all the tell-tale signs of very rapid writing. It is with great pleasure that I commend this revision to readers old and new in the certainty that William Barclay speaks even more clearly to us all with his wonderful appeal in this new version of his much-loved *Daily Study Bible*.

Ronnie Barclay
Bedfordshire
2001

GENERAL INTRODUCTION

(by William Barclay, from the 1975 edition)

The Daily Study Bible series has always had one aim – to convey the results of scholarship to the ordinary reader. A. S. Peake delighted in the saying that he was a 'theological middle-man', and I would be happy if the same could be said of me in regard to these volumes. And yet the primary aim of the series has never been academic. It could be summed up in the famous words of Richard of Chichester's prayer – to enable men and women 'to know Jesus Christ more clearly, to love him more dearly, and to follow him more nearly'.

It is all of twenty years since the first volume of *The Daily Study Bible* was published. The series was the brain-child of the late Rev. Andrew McCosh, MA, STM, the then Secretary and Manager of the Committee on Publications of the Church of Scotland, and of the late Rev. R. G. Macdonald, OBE, MA, DD, its Convener.

It is a great joy to me to know that all through the years *The Daily Study Bible* has been used at home and abroad, by minister, by missionary, by student and by layman, and that it has been translated into many different languages. Now, after so many printings, it has become necessary to renew the printer's type and the opportunity has been taken to restyle the books, to correct some errors in the text and to remove some references which have become outdated. At the same time, the Biblical quotations within the text have been changed to use the Revised Standard Version, but my own original translation of the New Testament passages has been retained at the beginning of each daily section.

There is one debt which I would be sadly lacking in courtesy if I did not acknowledge. The work of revision and correction has been done entirely by the Rev. James Martin, MA, BD, Minister of High Carntyne Church, Glasgow. Had it not been for him this task would never have been undertaken, and it is impossible for me to thank him enough for the selfless toil he has put into the revision of these books.

It is my prayer that God may continue to use *The Daily Study Bible* to enable men better to understand His word.

William Barclay
Glasgow
1975
(Published in the 1975 edition)

GENERAL FOREWORD
(by John Drane)

I only met William Barclay once, not long after his retirement from the chair of Biblical Criticism at the University of Glasgow. Of course I had known about him long before that, not least because his theological passion – the Bible – was also a significant formative influence in my own life and ministry. One of my most vivid memories of his influence goes back to when I was working on my own doctoral research in the New Testament. It was summer 1971, and I was a leader on a mission team working in the north-east of Scotland at the same time as Barclay's Baird Lectures were being broadcast on national television. One night, a young Ph.D. scientist who was interested in Christianity, but still unsure about some things, came to me and announced: 'I've just been watching William Barclay on TV. He's convinced me that I need to be a Christian; when can I be baptized?' That kind of thing did not happen every day. So how could it be that Barclay's message was so accessible to people with no previous knowledge or experience of the Christian faith?

I soon realised that there was no magic ingredient that enabled this apparently ordinary professor to be a brilliant communicator. His secret lay in who he was, his own sense of identity and purpose, and above all his integrity in being true to himself and his faith. Born in the far north of Scotland, he was brought up in Motherwell, a steel-producing town south of Glasgow where his family settled when he was only five, and this was the kind of place where he felt most at home. Though his association with the University of Glasgow provided a focus for his life over almost fifty years, from his first day as a student in 1925 to his retirement from the faculty in 1974, he never became an ivory-tower academic, divorced from the realities of life in the real world. On the contrary, it was his commitment to the working-class culture of industrial Clydeside that enabled him to make such a lasting contribution not only to the world of the university but also to the life of the Church.

He was ordained to the ministry of the Church of Scotland at the age of twenty-six, but was often misunderstood even by other Christians. I doubt that William Barclay would ever have chosen words such as 'missionary' or 'evangelist' to describe his own ministry, but he accomplished what few others have done, as he took the traditional Presbyterian emphasis on spirituality-through-learning and transformed it into a most effective vehicle for evangelism. His own primary interest was in the history and language of the New Testament, but William Barclay was never only a historian or literary critic. His constant concern was to explore how these ancient books, and the faith of which they spoke, could continue to be relevant to people of his own time. If the Scottish churches had known how to capitalize on his enormous popularity in the media during the 1960s and 1970s, they might easily have avoided much of the decline of subsequent years.

Connecting the Bible to life has never been the way to win friends in the world of academic theology, and Barclay could undoubtedly have made things easier for himself had he been prepared to be a more conventional academic. But he was too deeply rooted in his own culture – and too seriously committed to the gospel – for that. He could see little purpose in a belief system that was so wrapped up in arcane and complicated terminology that it was accessible only to experts. Not only did he demystify Christian theology, but he also did it for working people, addressing the kind of things that mattered to ordinary folks in their everyday lives. In doing so, he also challenged the elitism that has often been deeply ingrained in the twin worlds of academic theology and the Church, with their shared assumption that popular culture is an inappropriate vehicle for serious thinking. Professor Barclay can hardly have been surprised when his predilection for writing books for the masses – not to mention talking to them on television – was questioned by his peers and even occasionally dismissed as being 'unscholarly' or insufficiently 'academic'. That was all untrue, of course, for his work was soundly based in reliable scholarship and his own extensive knowledge of the original languages of the Bible. But like One many centuries before him (and unlike most of his peers, in both Church and academy), 'the common people heard him gladly' (Mark 12:37), which no doubt explains why his writings are still inspirational – and why it is a particular pleasure for me personally to commend them to a new readership in a new century.

John Drane
University of Aberdeen
2001

EDITOR'S PREFACE

(by Linda Foster)

When the first volume of the original *Daily Bible Readings*, which later became *The Daily Study Bible* (the commentary on Acts), was published in 1953, no one could have anticipated or envisaged the revolution in the use of language which was to take place in the last quarter of the twentieth century. Indeed, when the first revised edition, to which William Barclay refers in his General Introduction, was completed in 1975, such a revolution was still waiting in the wings. But at the beginning of the twenty-first century, inclusive language and the concept of political correctness are well-established facts of life. It has therefore been with some trepidation that the editing of this unique and much-loved text has been undertaken in producing *The New Daily Study Bible*. Inevitably, the demands of the new language have resulted in the loss of some of Barclay's most sonorous phrases, perhaps best remembered in the often-repeated words 'many a man'. Nonetheless, this revision is made in the conviction that William Barclay, the great communicator, would have welcomed it. In the discussion of Matthew 9:16–17 ('The Problem of the New Idea'), he affirmed the value of language that has stood the test of time and in which people have 'found comfort and put their trust', but he also spoke of 'living in a changing and expanding world' and questioned the wisdom of reading God's word to twentieth-century men and women in Elizabethan English. It is the intention of this new edition to heed that warning and to bring

William Barclay's message of God's word to readers of the twenty-first century in the language of their own time.

In the editorial process, certain decisions have been made in order to keep a balance between that new language and the familiar Barclay style. Quotations from the Bible are now taken from the New Revised Standard Version, but William Barclay's own translation of individual passages has been retained throughout. Where the new version differs from the text on which Barclay originally commented, because of the existence of an alternative reading, the variant text is indicated by square brackets. I have made no attempt to guess what Barclay would have said about the NRSV text; his commentary still refers to the Authorized (King James) and Revised Standard Versions of the Bible, but I believe that the inclusive language of the NRSV considerably assists the flow of the discussion.

For similar reasons, the dating conventions of BC and AD – rather than the more recent and increasingly used BCE (before the common era) and CE (common era) – have been retained. William Barclay took great care to explain the meanings of words and phrases and scholarly points, but it has not seemed appropriate to select new terms and make such explanations on his behalf.

One of the most difficult problems to solve has concerned monetary values. Barclay had his own system for translating the coinage of New Testament times into British currency. Over the years, these equivalent values have become increasingly out of date, and often the force of the point being made has been lost or diminished. There is no easy way to bring these equivalents up to date in a way that will continue to make sense, particularly when readers come from both sides of the Atlantic. I have therefore followed the only known yardstick that gives any feel for the values concerned, namely that a *denarius* was a day's wage for a working man, and I have made alterations to the text accordingly.

One of the striking features of *The Daily Study Bible* is the range of quotations from literature and hymnody that are used by way of illustration. Many of these passages appeared without identification or attribution, and for the new edition I have attempted wherever possible to provide sources and authors. In the same way, details have been included about scholars and other individuals cited, by way of context and explanation, and I am most grateful to Professor John Drane for his assistance in discovering information about some of the more obscure or unfamiliar characters. It is clear that readers use *The Daily Study Bible* in different ways. Some look up particular passages while others work through the daily readings in a more systematic way. The descriptions and explanations are therefore not offered every time an individual is mentioned (in order to avoid repetition that some may find tedious), but I trust that the information can be discovered without too much difficulty.

Finally, the 'Further Reading' lists at the end of each volume have been removed. Many new commentaries and individual studies have been added to those that were the basis of William Barclay's work, and making a selection from that ever-increasing catalogue is an impossible task. It is nonetheless my hope that the exploration that begins with these volumes of *The New Daily Study Bible* will go on in the discovery of new writers and new books.

Throughout the editorial process, many conversations have taken place – conversations with the British and American publishers, and with those who love the books and find in them both information and inspiration. Ronnie Barclay's contribution to this revision of his father's work has been invaluable. But one conversation has dominated the work, and that has been a conversation with William Barclay himself through the text. There has been a real sense of listening to his voice in all the questioning and in the searching for new words to convey the meaning of that text. The aim of *The New Daily Study Bible* is to make clear his message, so that the distinctive voice, which has spoken to so many in past years, may continue to be heard for generations to come.

Linda Foster
London
2001

The Letters of John

INTRODUCTION TO THE
FIRST LETTER OF JOHN

A Personal Letter and its Background

The First Letter of John is called a letter, but it has no opening address nor closing greetings such as the letters of Paul have. And yet no one can read it without feeling its intensely personal character. Beyond all doubt, the man who wrote it had in his mind's eye a definite situation and a definite group of people. Both the form and the personal character of 1 John will be explained if we think of it as what someone has called 'a loving and anxious sermon', written by a pastor who loved his people, and sent out to the various churches over which he had charge.

Any such letter is produced by an actual situation apart from which it cannot be fully understood. If we wish to understand 1 John, we have first of all to try to reconstruct the situation which produced it, remembering that it was written in Ephesus a little after AD 100.

The Falling Away

By AD 100, certain things had almost inevitably happened within the Church, especially in a place like Ephesus.

(1) Many were now second- or even third-generation Christians. The thrill of the first days had, to some extent at least, passed away. In 'The Prelude', Wordsworth said of one of the great moments of modern history:

3

Bliss was it in that dawn to be alive.

In the first days of Christianity, there was a glory and a splendour; but now Christianity had become a thing of habit, 'traditional, half-hearted, nominal'. People had grown used to it, and something of the wonder had been lost. Jesus knew human nature, and he had said: 'The love of many will grow cold' (Matthew 24:12). John was writing at a time when, for some at least, the first thrill had gone and the flame of devotion had died to a flicker.

(2) One result was that there were members of the Church who found that the standards which Christianity demanded were becoming a burden and who were tired of making the effort. They did not want to be *saints* in the New Testament sense of the term. The New Testament word for *saint* is *hagios*, which is also commonly translated as *holy*. Its basic meaning is *different*. The Temple was *hagios* because it was *different* from other buildings; the Sabbath was *hagios* because it was *different* from other days; the Jewish nation was *hagios* because it was *different* from other nations; and Christians were called to be *hagios* because they were called to be *different* from other men and women. There was always a distinct division between Christians and the world. In the Fourth Gospel, Jesus says: 'If you belonged to the world, the world would love you as its own. Because you do not belong to the world, but I have chosen you out of the world – therefore the world hates you' (John 15:19). 'I have given them your word,' said Jesus in his prayer to God, 'and the world has hated them because they do not belong to the world, just as I do not belong to the world' (John 17:14).

All of this involved an ethical demand. It demanded a new standard of moral purity, a new kindness, a new service, a new forgiveness – and it was difficult. And, once the first thrill and enthusiasm were gone, it became harder and harder to stand out against the world and to refuse to conform to the generally accepted standards and practices of the age.

(3) It is to be noted that 1 John shows no signs that the church to which it was written was being persecuted. The peril, as it has been put, was not persecution but seduction; it came from within. That, too, Jesus had foreseen. 'Many false prophets', he said, 'will arise, and lead many astray' (Matthew 24:11). This was a danger of which Paul had warned the leaders of this very church of Ephesus when he made his farewell address to them. 'I know', he said, 'that after I have gone, savage wolves will come in among you, not sparing the flock. Some even from your own group will come distorting the truth in order to entice the disciples to follow them' (Acts 20:29–30).

The trouble which 1 John seeks to combat came not from people who were out to destroy the Christian faith but from those who thought they were improving it. It came from people whose aim was to make Christianity intellectually respectable. They knew the intellectual trends and currents of the day, and felt that the time had come for Christianity to come to terms with secular philosophy and contemporary thought.

The Contemporary Philosophy

What, then, was this contemporary thought and philosophy with which the false prophets and mistaken teachers wished to align the Christian faith? Throughout the Greek world, there was a way of thinking to which the general name of Gnosticism is given. The basic belief of all Gnostic thought was that only spirit was good and that matter, the material world, was essentially evil. The Gnostics, therefore, inevitably despised the world since it was matter. In particular, they despised the body, which, being matter, was necessarily evil. Imprisoned within this body was the human spirit. That spirit was a seed of God, who was altogether good. So, the aim of life must be to release this heavenly seed imprisoned in the evil of the body. That could be done only by a secret knowledge and elaborate ritual which only true Gnostics could supply. Here was a train of thought which was written deep into Greek thinking – and which has not even now ceased to exist. Its basis is the conviction that all matter is evil and that spirit alone is good, and that the one real aim in life is to liberate the human spirit from the vile prison house of the body.

The False Teachers

With that in our minds, let us turn to 1 John and gather the evidence as to who these false teachers were and what they taught. They had been within the Church, but they had withdrawn from it. 'They went out from us, but they did not belong to us' (1 John 2:19). They were people of influence, for they claimed to be prophets. 'Many false prophets have gone out into the world' (1 John 4:1). Although they had left the Church, they still tried to disseminate their teaching within it and to deceive its members and lead them away from the true faith (1 John 2:26).

The Denial of Jesus' Messiahship

At least some of these false teachers denied that Jesus was the Messiah. 'Who is the liar', demands John, 'but the one who denies that Jesus is the Christ?' (1 John 2:22). It is most likely that these false teachers were not Gnostics in the true sense of the word, but Jews. Things had always been difficult for Jewish Christians, but the events of history made them doubly so. It was very difficult for Jews to come to believe in a crucified Messiah. But suppose they had begun to believe this, their difficulties were by no means finished. The Christians believed that Jesus would return quickly to vindicate his people. Clearly, that would be a hope that would be specially dear to the hearts of the Jews. Then, in AD 70, Jerusalem was captured by the Romans, who were so infuriated with the long intransigence and the suicidal resistance of the Jews that they tore the holy city stone from stone and drew a plough across the middle of it. In view of that, how could the Jews easily accept the hope that Jesus would come and save them? The holy city was desolate; the Jews were dispersed throughout the world. In view of that, how could it be true that the Messiah had come?

The Denial of the Incarnation

There was something even more serious than that. There was false teaching which came directly from an attempt from within the Church to bring Christianity into line with Gnosticism. We must remember the Gnostic point of view that spirit alone was good and matter utterly evil. *Given that point of view, any real incarnation is impossible*. That is exactly what, centuries later, St Augustine was to point out. Before he became a Christian, he was skilled in the philosophies of the various schools. In the *Confessions* (8:9), he tells us that somewhere in the writings of the Platonists he had read in one form or another nearly all the things that Christianity says; but there was one great Christian saying which he had never found in any of these works and which no one would ever find – and that saying was: 'The Word became flesh and lived among us' (John 1:14). Since these thinkers believed in the essential evil of matter and therefore the essential evil of the body, that was one thing they could never say.

It is clear that the false teachers against whom John was writing in this First Letter denied the reality of the incarnation and of Jesus' physical body. 'Every spirit', writes John, 'that confesses that Jesus Christ has come in the flesh is from God, and every spirit that does not confess Jesus is not from God' (1 John 4:2–3).

In the early Church, this refusal to admit the reality of the incarnation took, broadly speaking, two forms.

(1) In its more radical and wholesale form, it was called *Docetism*, which the scholar E. J. Goodspeed suggests might be translated as *Seemism*. The Greek verb *dokein* means *to seem*; and the Docetists taught that Jesus only *seemed* to have a body. They insisted that he was a purely spiritual being who had nothing but the appearance of having a body. One of the apocryphal books written from this point of view is the Acts of John, which dates from about AD 160. In it, John is made to say that sometimes when he touched Jesus he seemed to meet with a material body, but at other times 'the substance was immaterial, as if it did not exist at all', and also that, when Jesus walked, he never left any footprint upon the ground. The simplest form of Docetism is the complete denial that Jesus ever had a physical body.

(2) There was a more subtle, and perhaps more dangerous, variant of this theory connected with the name of Cerinthus. In tradition, John and Cerinthus were sworn enemies. The great early Church historian Eusebius (*Ecclesiastical History*, 4:14:6) hands down a story which tells how John went to the public bathhouse in Ephesus to bathe. He saw Cerinthus inside and refused even to enter the building. 'Let us flee,' he said, 'lest even the bathhouse fall, because Cerinthus the enemy of truth is within.' Cerinthus drew a definite distinction between the human Jesus and the divine Christ. He said that Jesus was a man, born in a perfectly natural way. He lived in special

obedience to God, and after his baptism the Christ in the shape of a dove descended upon him, from that power which is above all powers, and then he brought news of the Father who up to that point had been unknown. Cerinthus did not stop there. He said that, at the end of Jesus' life, the Christ again withdrew from him so that the Christ never suffered at all. It was the human Jesus who suffered, died and rose again.

This again comes out in the stories of the apocryphal gospels written under the influence of this point of view. In the Gospel of Peter, written in about AD 130, it is said that Jesus showed no pain upon the cross and that his cry was: 'My power! My power! Why have you forsaken me?' It was at that moment that the divine Christ left the human Jesus. The Acts of John go further. They tell how, when the human Jesus was being crucified on Calvary, John was actually talking to the divine Christ in a cave in the hillside and that the Christ said to him: 'John, to the multitude down below in Jerusalem I am being crucified, and pierced with lances and with reeds, and gall and vinegar are given me to drink. But I am speaking to you, and listen to what I say . . . Nothing, therefore, of the things they will say of me have I suffered' (Acts of John 97).

We may see from the Letters of Ignatius how widespread this way of thinking was. Ignatius was writing to a group of churches in Asia Minor which must have been much the same as the group to which 1 John was written. When Ignatius wrote, he was a prisoner and was being transported to Rome to be martyred by being flung to the wild animals in the arena. He wrote to the Trallians: 'Be deaf, therefore, when anyone speaks to you apart from Jesus Christ, who was of the family of David and Mary, who was truly born, both ate and drank, was truly persecuted under Pontius Pilate, was truly crucified and died . . . who also was truly raised from the dead . . . But if, as some affirm, who are without God – that is, who are unbelievers – his suffering was only a semblance . . . why am I a prisoner?' (Ignatius, *To the Trallians*, 9–10). To the Christians at Smyrna, he wrote: 'For he suffered all these things for us that we might attain salvation, and he truly suffered even as he also truly raised himself, not as some unbelievers say that his passion was merely in semblance' (*To the Smyrnaeans*, 2). Polycarp, writing to the Philippians, used John's very words: 'For everyone who does not confess that Jesus Christ has come in the flesh is an anti-Christ' (*To the Philippians*, 7:1).

This teaching of Cerinthus is also rebuked in 1 John. John writes of Jesus: 'This is the one who came by water and blood, Jesus Christ, *not with the water only but with the water and the blood*' (1 John 5:6). The point of that verse is that the Gnostic teachers would have agreed that the divine Christ came by *water*, that is, at the baptism of Jesus; but they would have denied that he came by *blood*, that is, by the cross, for they insisted that the divine Christ left the human Jesus before his crucifixion.

The great danger of this heresy is that it comes from what can only be called a mistaken reverence. It is afraid to ascribe to Jesus full humanity. It regards it as irreverent to think that he had a truly physical body. It is a heresy which is by no means dead but is still held today, usually quite unconsciously, by many devout Christians. But it must be remembered, as John so clearly saw, that our salvation was dependent on the full identification of Jesus Christ with us. As one of the great early Church fathers unforgettably put it, 'He became what we are to make us what he is.'

This Gnostic belief had certain practical consequences in the lives of those who held it.

(1) The Gnostic attitude to matter and to all created things produced a certain attitude to the body and the things to do with the body. That attitude might take any one of three different forms.

(a) It might take the form of self-denial, with fasting and celibacy and rigid control, even deliberate ill-treatment, of the body. The view that celibacy is better than marriage and that sex is sinful goes back to Gnostic influence and belief – and this is a view which still lingers on in certain quarters. There is no trace of that view in this letter.

(b) It might take the form of an assertion that the body did not matter and that, therefore, its appetites might be satisfied without restraint. Since the body was in any event evil, it made no difference what was done with it. There are echoes of this in this letter. John condemns as liars all who say that they know God and yet do not keep God's commandments; those who say that they abide in Christ ought to walk as Christ walked (1 John 1:6, 2:4–6). There were clearly Gnostics in these communities who claimed special knowledge of God but whose conduct was a long way from the demands of the Christian ethic.

In certain quarters, this Gnostic belief went even further. Gnostics were people who had *gnōsis*, *knowledge*. Some held that real Gnostics must, therefore, know the best as well as the worst and must enter into every experience of life at its highest or at its deepest level, as the case may be. It might almost be said that such people held that it was an obligation to sin. There is a reference to this kind of belief in the letter to Thyatira in the book of Revelation, where the risen Christ refers to those who have known 'the deep things of Satan' (Revelation 2:24). And it may well be that John is referring to these people when he insists that 'God is light and in him there is no darkness at all' (1 John 1:5). These particular

Gnostics would have held that there was in God not only blazing light but also deep darkness – and that an individual must penetrate both. It is easy to see the disastrous consequences of such a belief.

(c) There was a third kind of Gnostic belief. True Gnostics regarded themselves as spiritual people in every sense, as having shed all the material things of life and released their spirits from the bondage of matter. Such Gnostics held that they were so spiritual that they were above and beyond sin and had reached spiritual perfection. It is to them that John refers when he speaks of those who deceive themselves by saying that they have no sin (1 John 1:8–10).

Whichever of these three forms Gnostic belief took, its ethical consequences were perilous in the extreme; and it is clear that the last two forms were to be found in the society to which John wrote.

(2) Further, this Gnosticism resulted in an attitude to men and women which inevitably destroyed Christian fellowship. We have seen that Gnostics aimed at the release of the spirit from the prison house of the evil body by means of an elaborate and mysterious knowledge. Clearly, such a knowledge was not for everyone. Ordinary people were too involved in the everyday life and work of the world ever to have time for the study and discipline necessary; and, even if they had had the time, many were intellectually incapable of grasping the involved speculations of Gnostic theosophy and so-called philosophy.

This produced an inevitable result. It divided people into two classes – those who were capable of a really spiritual life, and those who were not. In the ancient world, every individual was thought of as consisting of three parts. There was the *sōma*, the *body*, the physical part. There was the *psuchē*, which is often translated as *soul*; but we must be careful, because it does not mean what we mean by *soul*. To the Greeks, the *psuchē* was the principle of physical life. Everything which had physical life had *psuchē*. *Psuchē* was the life principle which human beings shared with all living creatures. Finally, there was the *pneuma*, the spirit; and it was the spirit which was possessed only by human beings and which made them kin to God.

The aim of Gnosticism was the release of the *pneuma* from the *sōma*; but that release could be won only by long and arduous study which only the intellectuals who had time on their hands could ever undertake. The Gnostics, therefore, divided people into two classes – the *psuchikoi*, who could never advance beyond the principle of physical life and never attain to anything else than what was to all intents and purposes animal living; and the *pneumatikoi*, who were truly spiritual and truly akin to God.

The result was clear. The Gnostics produced a spiritual aristocracy who looked with contempt and even hatred on lesser mortals. The *pneumatikoi* regarded the *psuchikoi* as contemptible, earthbound creatures who could never know what real religion was. The consequence was obviously the annihilation of Christian fellowship. That is why John insists throughout his letter that the true test of Christianity is love for one another. If we really are walking in the light, we have fellowship with one another (1:7). Whoever claims to be in the light and hates a fellow Christian is in fact in darkness (2:9–11). The proof that we have passed from dark to light is that we love each other (3:14–17). The marks of Christianity are belief in Christ and love for one another (3:23). God is love, and whoever does not love does not know God at all (4:7–8). Because God loved us, we ought to love each other; it is when we love each other that God dwells in us (4:10–12). The commandment is that those who love God must love their brothers and sisters also, and those who say they love God and at the same time hate their brothers and sisters are branded as liars (4:20–1). The Gnostics, to put it bluntly, would have said that the mark of true religion is contempt for ordinary men and women; John insists in every chapter that the mark of true religion is love for everyone.

Here, then, is a picture of these Gnostic heretics. They talked of being born of God, of walking in the light, of having no sin, of dwelling in God, of knowing God. These were their catchphrases. They had no intention of destroying the Church and the faith; by their way of thinking, they were going to cleanse the Church of dead wood and make Christianity an intellectually respectable philosophy, fit to stand beside the great systems of the day. But the effect of their teaching was to deny the incarnation, to eliminate the Christian ethic and to make fellowship within the Church impossible. It is little wonder that John seeks, with such fervent pastoral devotion, to defend the churches he loved from such an insidious attack from within. This was a threat far more perilous than any persecution from outside; the very existence of the Christian faith was at stake.

The Message of John

The First Letter of John is a short letter, and we cannot look within it for a systematic exposition of the Christian faith. Nonetheless, it will be of the greatest interest to examine the basic underlying beliefs with which John confronts those threatening to wreck the Christian faith.

The Object of Writing

John's object in writing is twofold; yet the two aspects are one and the same. He writes that the joy of his people may be completed (1:4), and that they may not sin (2:1). He sees clearly that, however attractive the wrong way may be, it is not in its nature to bring happiness. To bring his people joy and to preserve them from sin are one and the same thing.

The Idea of God

John has two great things to say about God. God is light, and in him there is no darkness at all (1:5). God is love, and that made him love us before we loved him, and made him send his Son as a remedy for our sins (4:7–10, 16). John's conviction is that God is self-revealing and self-giving. He is light, and not darkness; he is love, and not hate.

The Idea of Jesus

Because the main attack of the false teachers was on the person of Christ, this letter, which is concerned to answer them, is specially rich and helpful in what it has to say about him.

(1) Jesus is the one who was from the beginning (1:1, 2:14). When we are confronted with Jesus, we are confronted with the eternal.

(2) Another way of putting this is to say that Jesus is the Son of God, and for John it is essential to be convinced of that (4:15, 5:5). The relationship of Jesus to God is unique, and in him is seen God's ever-seeking and ever-forgiving heart.

(3) Jesus is the Christ, the Messiah (2:22, 5:1). That again, for him, is an essential article of belief. It may seem that here we come into a region of ideas which is much narrower and, in fact, specifically Jewish. But there is something essential here. To say that Jesus is from the beginning and that he is the Son of God is to preserve his connection with *eternity*; to say that he is the Messiah is to preserve his connection with *history*. It is to see his coming as the event towards which

God's plan, working itself out in his chosen people, was moving.

(4) Jesus was most truly and fully human. To deny that Jesus came in the flesh is to be moved by the spirit of antichrist (4:2–3). It is John's witness that Jesus was so truly human that he himself had known and touched him with his own hands (1:1–3). No writer in the New Testament holds with greater intensity the full reality of the incarnation. Not only did Jesus become a man, he also suffered for men and women. It was by water and blood that he came (5:6); and he laid down his life for us (3:16).

(5) The coming of Jesus, his incarnation, his life, his death, his resurrection and his ascension all combine to deal with human sin. Jesus was without sin (3:5); and human beings are essentially sinners, even though in our arrogance we may claim to be without sin (1:8–10); and yet the sinless one came to take away the sin of sinning humanity (3:5). In regard to our sin, Jesus is two things.

(a) He is our *advocate* with the Father (2:1). The word is *paraklētos*. A *paraklētos* is someone who is called in to help. The word could be used of a physician; it was often used of a witness called in to give evidence in favour of someone on trial, or of a defending lawyer called in to defend someone accused of an offence. Jesus pleads our case with God; he, the sinless one, is the defender of sinning men and women.

(b) But Jesus is more than that. Twice, John calls him the *expiation* for our sins (2:2, 4:10). When we sin, the relationship which should exist between us and God is broken. An expiatory sacrifice is one which restores that relationship; or, rather, it is a sacrifice through which that relationship is restored. It is an *atoning* sacrifice, a sacrifice which once again puts us *at one* with God. So, through what Jesus was and did, the relationship between God and all people, broken by sin, is restored. Jesus does not only plead the case of sinners; he sets them at one with God. The blood of Jesus Christ cleanses us from all sin (1:7).

(6) As a result of all this, through Jesus Christ, all who believe have life (4:9, 5:11–12). This is true in a double sense. Believers have life in the sense that they are saved from death; and they have life in the sense that living has ceased to be mere existence and has become life in its fullest sense.

(7) All this may be summed up by saying that Jesus is the Saviour of the world (4:14). Here, we have something which has to be set out in full. 'The Father has sent his Son as the Saviour of the world' (4:14). We have already talked of Jesus as pleading our case before God. If we were to leave that without addition, it might be argued that God wished to condemn human beings and was deflected from his dire purpose by the self-sacrifice of Jesus Christ. But that is not so, because, for John, as for every writer in the New Testament, the whole initiative lay with God. It was God who sent his Son to be the Saviour of men and women.

Within the short span of this letter, the wonder and the glory and the grace of Christ are most fully set out.

The Spirit

In this letter, John has less to say about the Spirit; for his highest teaching about the Spirit, we must turn back to the Fourth Gospel. It may be said that, in 1 John, the function of the Spirit is in some sense to be the liaison between God and his people. It is the Spirit who makes us conscious that there is within us the abiding presence of God through Jesus Christ (3:24, 4:13). We may say that it is the Spirit who enables us to grasp the precious fellowship with God which is being offered to us.

The World

The world within which Christians live is hostile; it is a world without God. It does not know Christians, because it did not know Christ (3:1). It hates Christians, just as it hated Christ (3:13). The false teachers are from the world and not from God, and it is because they speak its language that the world is ready to hear them and accept them (4:4–5). In a sweeping statement, John says that the whole world is in the power of the evil one (5:19). It is for that reason that Christians have to overcome it, and their weapon in the struggle with the world is faith (5:4).

Hostile as the world is, it is doomed. The world and all its desires are passing away (2:17). That, indeed, is why it is folly to give one's heart to the world; the world is coming to an end. Although Christians live in a hostile world which is passing away, there is no need for despair and fear. The darkness is past; the true light now shines (2:8). God in Christ has broken into time; the new age has come. It is not yet fully brought to fruition, but the consummation is sure.

Christians live in an evil and a hostile world, but they possess the means to overcome it; and, when the destined end of the world comes, they will be safe, because they already possess that which makes them members of the new community in the new age.

The Fellowship of the Church

John does more than move in the high realms of theology; he has certain most practical things to say about the Christian Church and the Christian life. No New Testament writer stresses more consistently or more strenuously the necessity of Christian fellowship. Christians, John was convinced, are not only bound to God; they are also bound to each other.

When we walk in the light, we have fellowship with each other (1:7). Those who claim to walk in the light but who hate their brothers and sisters are in reality walking in darkness; those who love their brothers and sisters are the ones who are in the light (2:9–11). The proof that people have passed from darkness to light is the fact that they love one another. To hate a fellow human being is in essence to be a murderer, as Cain was. If we are able out of our own wealth to help another's poverty and do not do so, it is ridiculous for us to claim that the love of God dwells in us. The essence of religion is to believe in the name of the Lord Jesus Christ and to love one another (3:11–17, 3:23). God is love; and, therefore, those who love are kin to God. God has loved us, and that is the best reason for loving each other (4:7–12). If we say that we love God and at the same time hate another person, we are liars. The command is that all who love God must love others too (4:20–1).

It was John's conviction that the only way in which anyone can prove love for God is by loving other people, and that that love must be not only a sentimental emotion but also a dynamic towards practical help.

Christian Righteousness

No New Testament writer makes a stronger ethical demand than John, or more strongly condemns a so-called religion which fails to produce ethical action. God is righteous, and the life of everyone who knows him must reflect his righteousness (2:29). Whoever abides in Christ, and is born of God, does not sin; whoever does not do right is not of God (3:3–10); and the characteristic of this righteousness is that it translates into love for other people (3:10–11). We show our love to God and to others by keeping God's commandments (5:2). Whoever is born of God does not sin (5:18).

For John, knowledge of God and obedience to him must always go hand in hand. It is by keeping his commandments that we prove that we really do know God. Those who say that they know him and who do not keep his commandments are liars (2:3–5).

It is, in fact, this obedience which is the basis of effective prayer. We receive what we ask from God because we keep his commandments and do what is pleasing in his sight (3:22).

The two marks which characterize genuine Christianity are love for one another and obedience to the revealed commandments of God.

The Destination of the Letter

There are certain baffling problems with regard to the letter's destination. The letter itself gives us no clue as to where it was sent. Tradition strongly connects it with Asia Minor, and especially with Ephesus, where, according to tradition, John lived for many years. But there are certain other odd facts which somehow have to be explained.

The sixth-century Roman historian Cassiodorus says that the First Letter of John was titled *Ad Parthos*, 'To the Parthians'; and St Augustine has a series of ten tractates written on the Epistle of John *ad Parthos*. One Geneva manuscript complicates the matter still further by titling the letter *Ad Sparthos*. There is no such word as *Sparthos*. There are two possible explanations of this impossible title. (1) Just possibly, what is meant is *Ad Sparsos*, which would mean 'to the Christians scattered abroad'. (2) In Greek, *Ad Parthos* would be *Pros Parthous*. Now, in the early manuscripts, there was no space between the words, and they were all written in capital letters, so that the title would run PROSPARTHOUS. A scribe writing to dictation could quite easily put that down as PROSSPARTHOUS, especially if he did not know what the title meant. *Ad Sparthos* can be eliminated as a mere mistake.

But where did 'To the Parthians' come from? There is one possible explanation. The Second Letter of John does tell us of its destination; it is written to *The elect lady and her children* (2 John 1). Let us turn to the end of 1 Peter. The Authorized Version has: 'The church that is at Babylon, elected together with you, saluteth you' (1 Peter 5:13). The phrase *the church that is* is printed in the Authorized Version in italics. This, of course, means that it has no equivalent in the Greek, which has, in fact, no actual mention of a *church* at all. This the Revised Standard Version accurately indicates: 'She who is at Babylon, who is likewise chosen [elect], sends you greetings.' As far as the Greek goes, it would be perfectly possible, and indeed natural, to take that as referring not to a *church* but to a *lady*. That is precisely what certain of the scholars in the very early Church did. Now, we find *the elect lady* again in 2 John. It was easy to identify the two elect ladies and to assume that 2 John was also written to Babylon. The natural title for the inhabitants of Babylon was Parthians, and hence we have the explanation of the title.

The process went even further. The Greek for *the elect lady* is *hē elektē*. We have already seen that the early manuscripts were written all in capital letters; and it would be just possible to take *Elektē* not as an adjective meaning *elect* but as a proper name, *Elekta*. This is, in fact, what the second-century theologian Clement of Alexandria may have done, for we have information that he said that the Johannine letters were written to a certain Babylonian lady, Elekta by name, and to her children.

So, it may well be that the title *Ad Parthos* arose from a series of misunderstandings. *The elect one* in 1 Peter is quite certainly the Church, as the Authorized Version rightly saw.

James Moffatt translates: 'Your sister church in Babylon, elect like yourselves, salutes you.' Further, it is almost certain that, in any event, *Babylon* there stands for *Rome*, which the early writers identified with Babylon, the great prostitute, drunk with the blood of the saints (cf. Revelation 17:5). The title *Ad Parthos* has a most interesting history; but clearly it arose from a simple misunderstanding.

There is one further complication. Clement of Alexandria referred to John's letters as 'written to virgins'. On the face of it, that is improbable, for it would not be a specially relevant title for them. How could that idea come about? The Greek would be *Pros Parthenous*, which closely resembles *Pros Parthous*; and, it so happens, John was regularly called *Ho Parthenos*, the Virgin, because he never married and because of the purity of his life. This further title must have come from a confusion between *Ad Parthos* and *Ho Parthenos*.

This is a case where we may take it that tradition is right and all the ingenious theories mistaken. We may take it that these letters were written in Ephesus and to the surrounding churches in Asia Minor. When John wrote, it would certainly be to the district for which he had oversight – and that was Ephesus and the surrounding territory. He is never mentioned in connection with Babylon.

In Defence of the Faith

John wrote his great letter to meet a threatening situation and in defence of the faith. The heresies which he attacked are by no means altogether echoes of what Wordsworth, in his poem 'The Solitary Reaper', called 'old unhappy far-off things and battles long ago'. They are still beneath the surface, and sometimes they even still raise their heads. To study his letter will confirm us in the true faith and enable us to have a defence against anything that would seduce us from it.

1 JOHN

THE PASTOR'S AIM

1 John 1:1-4

> What we are telling you about is that which was from
> the beginning, that which we heard, that which we saw
> with our eyes, that which we gazed upon, and which
> our hands touched. It is about the word of life that we
> are telling you. (And the life appeared to us, and we
> saw it, and testify to it; and we are now bringing you
> the message of this eternal life, which was with the
> Father and which appeared to us.) It is about what we
> saw and heard that we are bringing the message to you,
> that you too may have fellowship with us, for our
> fellowship is with the Father and with Jesus Christ, the
> Son. And we are writing these things to you that your
> joy may be completed.

EVERYONE who sits down to write a letter or gets up to preach
a sermon has some object in view. The intention, and the
hope, is to produce some effect in the minds and hearts and
lives of those to whom that message is addressed. And here,
at the very beginning of his letter, John sets down his aim in
writing to his people.

(1) It is his wish to produce fellowship with the community and fellowship with God (verse 3). The pastor's aim

23

must always be to bring people closer to one another and closer to God. Any message which encourages and leads to division is a false message. The Christian message can be summed up as having two great aims – love for one another and love for God.

(2) It is his wish to bring his people joy (verse 4). Joy is the essence of Christianity. A message whose only effect is to depress and to discourage those who hear it has stopped half-way. It is quite true that often the aim of the preacher and the teacher must be to awaken a godly sorrow which will lead to a true repentance. But, after the sense of sin has been produced, men and women must be led to the Saviour in whom sins are all forgiven. The ultimate note of the Christian message is joy.

(3) To that end, John's aim is to set Jesus Christ before them. One great teacher always used to tell his students that their one aim as preachers must be 'to speak a good word for Jesus Christ'; and it was said of another great man that, wherever his conversation began, it cut straight across country to Jesus Christ.

The simple fact is that, if we are ever to find fellowship with one another and fellowship with God, and if we are ever to find true joy, we must find them in Jesus Christ.

THE PASTOR'S RIGHT TO SPEAK

1 John 1:1–4 (*contd*)

HERE at the very beginning of his letter, John sets down his right to speak. It consists in one thing – in personal experience of Christ (verses 2–3).

(1) He says that he has *heard* Christ. Long ago, Zedekiah had said to Jeremiah: 'Is there any word from the Lord?'

(Jeremiah 37:17). What people are interested in is not someone's opinions and views, but a word from the Lord. It was said of one preacher that first he listened to God and then he spoke to men and women; and it was said of John Brown, the eighteenth-century minister of the Scottish town of Haddington, that, when he preached, he often paused as if listening for a voice. True teachers are those who have a message from Jesus Christ because they have heard his voice.

(2) He says that he has *seen* Christ. It is told of Alexander Whyte, the great Scottish preacher, that someone once said to him: 'You preached today as if you had come straight from the presence.' And Whyte answered: 'Perhaps I did.' We cannot see Christ in the flesh as John did; but we can still see him with the eye of faith. As J. G. Whittier's hymn 'Immortal love' has it,

> And, warm, sweet, tender, even yet
> A present help is he;
> And faith has still its Olivet,
> And love its Galilee.

(3) He says that he has *gazed* on Christ. What is the difference between *seeing* Christ and *gazing* upon him? In the Greek, the verb for *to see* is *horan*, and it means simply to see with physical sight. The verb for *to gaze* is *theasthai*, and it means to gaze at someone or something until something has been grasped of the significance of that person or thing. So Jesus, speaking to the crowds of John the Baptist, asked: 'What did you go out into the wilderness *to look at* [*theasthai*]?' (Luke 7:24); and in that word he describes how the crowds flocked out to gaze at John and wonder who and what this man might be. Speaking of Jesus in the prologue to his gospel, John says: 'We *have seen* his glory' (John 1:14).

The verb is again *theasthai*, and the idea is not that of a passing glance but of a steadfast searching gaze which seeks to discover something of the mystery of Christ.

(4) He says that his hands actually *touched* Christ. Luke tells of how Jesus came back to his disciples, when he had risen from the dead, and said: 'Look at my hands and my feet; see that it is I myself. Touch me and see; for a ghost does not have flesh and bones as you see that I have' (Luke 24:39). Here, John is thinking of those people called the Docetists who were so spiritually minded that they insisted that Jesus never had a flesh-and-blood body but was only a ghost in human form. They refused to believe that God could ever degrade himself by taking human flesh and blood upon himself. John here insists that the Jesus he had known was, in truth, a man who came among them; he felt there was nothing in all the world more dangerous – as we shall see – than to doubt that Jesus was fully human.

THE PASTOR'S MESSAGE

1 John 1:1–4 (*contd*)

JOHN's message is about Jesus Christ; and of Jesus he has three great things to say. First, he says that Jesus was *from the beginning*. That is to say, in him eternity entered time; in him the eternal God personally entered our world. Second, that entry into the world was a real entry; it was real humanity that God took upon himself. Third, through that action there came to men and women the word of life, the word which can change death into life and mere existence into real living. Again and again in the New Testament, the gospel is called a *word*; and it is of the greatest interest to see the various connections in which this term is used.

(1) More often than anything else, the gospel message is called the *word of God* (Acts 4:31, 6:2, 6:7, 11:1, 13:5, 13:7, 13:44, 16:32; Philippians 1:14; 1 Thessalonians 2:13; Hebrews 13:7; Revelation 1:2, 1:9, 6:9, 20:4). It is not a human discovery; it comes from God. It is news of God which men and women could not have discovered for themselves.

(2) Frequently, the gospel message is called the *word of the Lord* (Acts 8:25, 12:24, 13:49, 15:35; 1 Thessalonians 1:8; 2 Thessalonians 3:1). It is not always certain whether the Lord is God or Jesus, but more often than not it is Jesus who is meant. The gospel is, therefore, the message which God could have sent to men and women in no other way than through his Son.

(3) Twice, the gospel message is called the *word of hearing* (*logos akoēs*) (1 Thessalonians 2:13; Hebrews 4:2). That is to say, it depends on two things – on a voice ready to speak it and an ear ready to hear it.

(4) The gospel message is the *word of the kingdom* (Matthew 13:19). It is the announcement of the kingship of God and the summons to render to God the obedience which will make us citizens of that kingdom.

(5) The gospel message is the *word of the gospel* (Acts 15:7; Colossians 1:5). *Gospel* means *good news*; and the gospel is essentially the good news about God.

(6) The gospel is the *word of grace* (Acts 14:3, 20:32). It is the good news of God's generous and undeserved love for all; it is the news that we are not saddled with the impossible task of earning God's love but are freely offered it.

(7) The gospel is the *word of salvation* (Acts 13:26). It is the offer of forgiveness for past sin and of power to overcome sin in the future.

(8) The gospel is the *word of reconciliation* (2 Corinthians 5:19). It is the message that the lost relationship between

human beings and God is restored in Jesus Christ, who has broken down the barrier which sin had erected.

(9) The gospel is the *word of the cross* (I Corinthians 1:18). At the heart of the gospel is the cross, on which is shown to all the final proof of the forgiving, sacrificing, seeking love of God.

(10) The gospel is the *word of truth* (2 Corinthians 6:7; Ephesians 1:13; Colossians 1:5; 2 Timothy 2:15). With the coming of the gospel, it is no longer necessary to guess and feel our way in life, for Jesus Christ has brought to us the truth about God.

(11) The gospel is the *word of righteousness* (Hebrews 5:13). It is by the power of the gospel that we are enabled to break from the power of evil and to rise to the righteousness which is pleasing in the sight of God.

(12) The gospel is the *health-giving word* (2 Timothy 1:13, 2:8). It is the antidote which cures the poison of sin and the medicine which defeats the disease of evil.

(13) The gospel is the *word of life* (Philippians 2:16). It is through its power that we are delivered from death and enabled to enter into life at its best.

GOD IS LIGHT

1 John 1:5

> And this is the message which we have heard from him and which we pass on to you, that God is light, and there is no darkness in him.

IT is certainly the case that our individual characters will be determined by the character of the god whom we worship; and, therefore, John begins by laying down the nature of the God and Father of Jesus Christ whom Christians worship. God, he says, is light, and there is no darkness in him. What does this statement tell us about God?

(1) It tells us that he is splendour and glory. There is nothing so glorious as a blaze of light piercing the darkness. To say that God is light tells us of his sheer splendour.

(2) It tells us that God is self-revealing. Above all things, light is seen; and it lights up the darkness round about it. To say that God is light is to say that there is nothing secretive or furtive about him. He wishes to be seen and to be known.

(3) It tells us of God's purity and holiness. In God, there is none of the darkness which cloaks hidden evil. That he is light speaks to us of his white purity and stainless holiness.

(4) It tells us of the guidance of God. It is one of the great functions of light to show the way. The road that is lit is the road that can be seen clearly. To say that God is light is to say that he offers his guidance for the path we must tread.

(5) It tells us of the revealing quality in the presence of God. Light is the great revealer. Flaws and stains which are hidden in the shade are obvious in the light. Light reveals the imperfections in any piece of work or material. So, the imperfections of life are seen in the presence of God. As the poet and hymn-writer J. G. Whittier wrote,

> Our thoughts lie open to thy sight;
> And naked to thy glance;
> Our secret sins are in the light
> Of thy pure countenance.

We can never know either the depth to which life has fallen or the height to which it may rise until we see it in the revealing light of God.

THE HOSTILE DARK

1 John 1:5 (*contd*)

IN God, says John, there is no darkness at all. Throughout the New Testament, darkness stands for the very opposite of the Christian life.

(1) Darkness stands for the Christless life. It represents the life that people lived before they met Christ or the life that they live if they stray away from him. John writes to his people that, now that Christ has come, the darkness is past and the true light shines (1 John 2:8). Paul writes to his Christian friends that once they were darkness but now they are light in the Lord (Ephesians 5:8). God has delivered us from the power of darkness and brought us into the kingdom of his dear Son (Colossians 1:13). Christians are not in darkness, for they are children of the day (1 Thessalonians 5:4–5). Those who follow Christ shall not walk in darkness, as others must, but they will have the light of life (John 8:12). God has called the Christians out of darkness into his marvellous light (1 Peter 2:9).

(2) The dark is hostile to the light. In the prologue to his gospel, John writes that the light shines in the darkness, and the darkness has not overcome it (John 1:5). It is a picture of the darkness seeking to obliterate the light – but unable to overpower it. The dark and the light are natural enemies.

(3) The darkness stands for the ignorance of life apart from Christ. Jesus summons his friends to walk in the light so that the darkness does not overtake them, for those who walk in the darkness do not know where they are going (John 12:35). Jesus is the light, and he has come that those who believe in him should not walk in darkness (John 12:46). The dark stands for the essential lostness of life without Christ.

(4) The darkness stands for the chaos of life without God. God, says Paul, thinking of the first act of creation,

commanded his light to shine out of the darkness (2 Corinthians 4:6). Without God's light, the world is a chaos in which life has neither order nor sense.

(5) The darkness stands for the immorality of the Christless life. It is Paul's appeal to men and women that they should cast off the works of darkness (Romans 13:12). Because their deeds were evil, people loved the darkness rather than the light (John 3:19). The darkness stands for the way that the Christless life is filled with things which seek the shadows because they cannot stand the light.

(6) The darkness is characteristically unfruitful. Paul speaks of the unfruitful works of darkness (Ephesians 5:11). If growing things are deprived of the light, their growth is arrested. The darkness is the Christless atmosphere in which no fruit of the Spirit will ever grow.

(7) The darkness is connected with lovelessness and hate. If people hate one another, it is a sign that they walk in darkness (1 John 2:9–11). Love is sunshine, and hatred is the dark.

(8) The dark is the home of the enemies of Christ and the final goal of those who will not accept him. The struggle of Christians and of Christ is against the hostile rulers of the darkness of this world (Ephesians 6:12). Persistent and rebellious sinners are those for whom the mist of darkness is reserved (2 Peter 2:9; Jude 13). The darkness is the life which is separated from God.

THE NECESSITY OF WALKING IN THE LIGHT

1 John 1:6–7

If we say that we have fellowship with him and at the same time walk in darkness, we lie and are not doing

> the truth. But if we walk in the light, as he is in the
> light, we have fellowship with each other, and the blood
> of Jesus Christ is steadily cleansing us from all sin.

HERE, John is writing to counteract one heretical way of thought. There were those who claimed to be specially intellectually and spiritually advanced, but whose lives showed no sign of it. They claimed to have advanced so far along the road of knowledge and of spirituality that, for them, sin had ceased to matter and the laws had ceased to exist. Napoleon once said that laws were made for ordinary people but were never meant for the likes of him. So, these heretics claimed to be so advanced in their thinking that, even if they did sin, it was of no importance whatsoever. In the later years of the second century, Clement of Alexandria tells us that there were heretics who said that it made no difference how people lived. The second-century theologian Irenaeus tells us that they declared that truly spiritual people were quite incapable of ever being affected or harmed by sin, no matter what they did.

In answer, John insists on certain things.

(1) He insists that, to have fellowship with the God who is light, we must walk in the light, and that, if we are still walking in the moral and ethical darkness of the Christless life, we cannot have that fellowship. This is precisely what the Old Testament had said centuries before. God said: 'You shall be holy, for I the Lord your God am holy' (Leviticus 19:2; cf. 20:7, 20:26). Those who would find fellowship with God are committed to a life of goodness which reflects God's goodness. The New Testament scholar C. H. Dodd writes: 'The Church is a society of people who, believing in a God of pure goodness, accept the obligation to be good like him.' This does not mean that we must be perfect before we can have fellowship with God; if that were the case, all of us would be shut out. But it does mean that we must spend our whole

lives in the awareness of our obligations, in the effort to fulfil them and in penitence when we fail. It will mean that we must never think that sin does not matter; it will mean that the nearer we come to God, the more terrible sin will be to us.

(2) He insists that these mistaken thinkers have the wrong idea of truth. He says that, if people who claim to be specially advanced still walk in darkness, they are not *doing* the truth. Exactly the same phrase is used in the Fourth Gospel, when it speaks of those who do what is true (John 3:21). This means that, for Christians, truth is never only intellectual; it is always moral. It is not something which exercises only the mind; it is something which exercises the whole personality. Truth is not only the discovery of abstract things; it is concrete living. It is not only thinking; it is also acting. The words which the New Testament uses along with *truth* are significant. It speaks of *obeying* the truth (Romans 2:8; Galatians 3:7), *following* the truth (Galatians 2:14; 3 John 4), *opposing* the truth (2 Timothy 3:8) and *wandering from* the truth (James 5:19). There is something that might be called 'discussion-group Christianity'. It is possible to look on Christianity as a series of intellectual problems to be solved, and on the Bible as a book about which illuminating information is to be gathered. But Christianity is something to be followed, and the Bible is a book to be obeyed. It is possible for intellectual superiority and moral failure to go hand in hand. For Christians, the truth is something first to be discovered and then to be obeyed.

THE TESTS OF TRUTH

1 John 1:6–7 (*contd*)

As John sees it, there are two great tests of truth.

(1) Truth is the creator of fellowship. If men and women are really walking in the light, they have fellowship with one

another. No belief can be fully Christian if it separates people from their neighbours. No church can be exclusive and still be the Church of Christ. Anything that destroys fellowship cannot be true.

(2) Those who really know the truth are each day more and more cleansed from sin by the blood of Jesus. The Revised Standard Version is correct enough here, but it can very easily be misunderstood. It runs: 'The blood of Jesus his Son cleanses us from all sin.' That can be read as a statement of a general principle. But it is a statement of what ought to be happening in the life of every individual. The meaning is that, all the time, day by day, constantly and consistently, the blood of Jesus Christ ought to be carrying out a cleansing process in the life of the individual Christian.

The Greek for *to cleanse* is *katharizein*, which was originally a ritual word, describing the ceremonies and washings and so on that qualified an individual to approach the gods. But, as religion developed, the word came to have a moral sense; and it describes the goodness which enables people to enter into the presence of God. So, what John is saying is: 'If you really know what the sacrifice of Christ has done and are really experiencing its power, day by day you will be adding holiness to your life and becoming more fit to enter the presence of God.'

Here indeed is a great conception. It looks on the sacrifice of Christ as something which not only atones for past sin but also equips people in holiness day by day.

True religion is the means by which every day we come closer to one another and closer to God. It produces fellowship with God and fellowship with other people – and we can never have the one without the other.

THE THREEFOLD LIE

1 John 1:6–7 (*contd*)

FOUR times in his letter, John bluntly accuses the false teachers of being liars; and the first of these occasions is in this passage.

(1) Those who claim to have fellowship with the God who is altogether light and yet who walk in the dark are lying (verse 6). A little later, he repeats this charge in a slightly different way. The one who claims to know God and yet does not keep God's commandments is a liar (1 John 2:4). John is laying down the blunt truth that those who say one thing with their lips and another thing with their lives are liars. He is not thinking of those who try their hardest and yet often fail. 'A man', said the writer H. G. Wells, 'may be a very bad musician, and may yet be passionately in love with music'; and we may be very conscious of our failures and yet be passionately in love with Christ and the way of Christ. John is thinking of those who make the highest possible claims to knowledge, to intellectual superiority and to spirituality, and who yet allow themselves things which they know very well are forbidden. Anyone who claims to love Christ and deliberately disobeys him is guilty of a lie.

(2) The one who denies that Jesus is the Christ is a liar (1 John 2:22). Here is something which runs through the whole New Testament. The ultimate test of any of us is our reaction to Jesus. The ultimate question which Jesus asks every one of us is: 'Who do you say that I am?' (Matthew 16:15). Confronted with Christ, we cannot but see the greatness that is there; and anyone who denies it is a liar.

(3) Anyone who claims to love God and at the same time hates another person is a liar (1 John 4:20). Love of God and hatred of others cannot exist in the same person. If there is bitterness in someone's heart towards any other, that is proof

that that person does not really love God. All our protestations
of love to God are useless if there is hatred in our hearts
towards anyone.

THE SINNER'S SELF-DECEPTION

1 John 1:8–10

> If we say that we have no sin, we deceive ourselves,
> and the truth is not in us. If we confess our sins, we can
> rely on him in his righteousness to forgive us our sins
> and to make us clean from all unrighteousness.
>   If we say that we have not sinned, we make him a
> liar, and his word is not in us.

In this passage, John describes and condemns two further
mistaken ways of thought.

(1) There are some people who say that they have no sin.
That may mean either of two things.

It may describe people who say that they have no responsibility for their sin. It is easy enough to find defences behind
which to seek to hide. We may blame our sins on our up-
bringing or on our genes, on our environment, on our tem-
perament or on our physical condition. We may claim that
someone misled us and that we were led astray. It is a human
characteristic that we seek to shuffle out of the responsibility
for sin. Or it may describe people who claim that they can sin
and come to no harm.

It is John's insistence that, when people have sinned,
excuses and self-justifications are irrelevant. The only thing
which will meet the situation is humble and penitent
confession to God and, if need be, to other people too.

Then John says a surprising thing. He says that we can
depend on God *in his righteousness* to forgive us if we confess

our sins. On the face of it, we might well have thought that God *in his righteousness* would have been much more likely to condemn than to forgive. But the point is that God, because he is righteous, never breaks his word; and Scripture is full of the promise of mercy to all who come to him with penitent hearts. God has promised that he will never despise the contrite heart and he will not break his word. If we humbly and sorrowfully confess our sins, he will forgive. The very fact of making excuses and looking for self-justification shuts us out from forgiveness, because it blocks our way to penitence; the very fact of humble confession opens the door to forgiveness, for those with penitent hearts can claim the promises of God.

(2) There are some people who say that they have not in fact sinned. That attitude is not nearly so uncommon as we might think. Any number of people do not really believe that they have sinned and rather resent being called sinners. Their mistake is that they think of sin as the kind of thing which gets into the news. They forget that sin is *hamartia*, which literally means a *missing of the target*. To fail to be as good a father, mother, wife, husband, son, daughter, employee or person as we might be is to sin; and that includes us all.

In any event, anyone who claims not to have sinned is in effect doing nothing less than calling God a liar, for God has said that all have sinned.

So, John condemns those who believe that they are so far advanced in knowledge and in the spiritual life that sin for them has ceased to matter; he condemns those who evade the responsibility for their sin or who hold that sin has no effect upon them; he condemns those who have never even realized that they are sinners. The essence of the Christian life is first to realize our sin and then to go to God for that forgiveness

37

which can wipe out the past and for that cleansing which can make the future new.

A PASTOR'S CONCERN

1 John 2:1–2

> My little children, I am writing these things to you that you may not sin. But, if anyone does sin, we have one who will plead our cause to the Father, Jesus Christ the righteous. For he is the propitiating sacrifice for our sins, and not for ours only but also for the whole world.

THE first thing to note in this passage is the sheer affection in it. John begins with the address: 'My little children'. Both in Latin and in Greek, diminutives carry a special affection. They are words which are used, as it were, with a caress. John is a very old man; he must be, in fact, the last survivor of his generation, maybe the last man alive who had walked and talked with Jesus in his days on earth. So often, age gets out of sympathy with youth and acquires even an impatient irritableness with the new and freer ways of the younger generation. But not John; in his old age, he has nothing but tenderness for those who are his little children in the faith. He is writing to tell them that they must not sin; but he does not scold. There is no edge in his voice; he seeks to love them into goodness. In this opening address, there is the yearning, affectionate tenderness of a pastor for people whom he has known for a long time in all their wayward foolishness, and whom he still loves.

His purpose in writing is to prevent them from sinning. There is a twofold connection of thought here – with what has gone before and with what comes afterwards. There is a twofold danger that they may indeed think lightly of sin.

John says two things about sin. First, he has just said that sin is universal; anyone who claims never to have sinned is a liar. Second, there is forgiveness of sins through what Jesus Christ has done, and still does, for men and women. Now, it would be possible to use both these statements as an excuse to take sin lightly. If all have sinned, why make a fuss about it, and what is the use of struggling against something which is, in any event, an inevitable part of the human situation? Again, if there is forgiveness of sins, why worry about it?

In response to that, John, as the New Testament scholar B. F. Westcott points out, has two things to say.

First, Christians are people who have come to know God; and the inevitable accompaniment of knowledge must be *obedience*. We shall return to this more fully; but, at the moment, we note that to know God and to obey God must, as John sees it, be twin parts of the same experience.

Second, those who claim that they abide in God (2:6) and in Jesus Christ must live the same kind of life as Jesus lived. That is to say, union with Christ necessarily involves *imitation* of Christ.

So, John lays down his two great ethical principles: knowledge involves obedience, and union involves imitation. Therefore, in the Christian life, there can never be any suggestion that sin should be taken lightly.

JESUS CHRIST OUR FRIEND AND DEFENDER

1 John 2:1–2 (*contd*)

IT will take us some considerable time to deal with these two verses, for in the New Testament there are few other verses which so concisely and clearly describe the work of Christ.

Let us first set out the problem. It is clear that Christianity is an ethical religion; that is what John is concerned to stress. But it is also clear that human beings are so often an ethical failure. Confronted with the demands of God, they acknowledge them and accept them – and then fail to keep them. Here, there is a barrier erected between us and God. How can we sinners ever enter into the presence of God, the all-holy? That problem is solved in Jesus Christ. And, in this passage, John uses two great words about Jesus Christ which we must study, not simply to acquire intellectual knowledge but to gain understanding and so to enter into the benefits of Christ.

He calls Jesus Christ our *advocate with the Father*. The word is *paraklētos*, which in the Fourth Gospel the Authorized Version translates as *comforter*. It is so great a word and has behind it so great a thought that we must examine it in detail. *Paraklētos* comes from the verb *parakalein*. There are occasions when *parakalein* means *to comfort*. It is, for instance, used with that meaning in Genesis 37:35, where it is said that all Jacob's sons and daughters rose up to *comfort* him at the loss of Joseph; in Isaiah 61:2, where it is said that the function of the prophet is to *comfort* all who mourn; and in Matthew 5:4, where it is said that those who mourn will be *comforted*.

But that is neither the most common nor the most literal sense of *parakalein*; its most usual meaning is *to call someone to one's side* in order to use that person in some way as a helper and a counsellor. In ordinary Greek, that is a very common usage. Xenophon, the Greek historian (*Anabasis*, 1:6:5), tells how the Persian emperor Cyrus the Younger *summoned* (*parakalein*) Clearchos into his tent to be his counsellor, for Clearchos was a man held in the highest honour by Cyrus and by the Greeks. Aeschines, the Greek orator, protests against his opponents calling in Demosthenes, his great rival, and says: 'Why need you *call* Demosthenes *to your support*? To do so is *to call in* a rascally rhetorician to cheat the ears of the jury' (*Against Ctesiphon*, 200).

Paraklētos itself is a word which is passive in form and literally means *someone who is called to one's side*; but, since it is always the reason for the calling in that is uppermost in the mind, the word, although passive in form, has an active sense, and comes to mean a helper, a supporter and, above all, a witness in someone's favour, an advocate in someone's defence. It is also a common word in ordinary secular Greek. The Athenian statesman Demosthenes (*De Falsa Legatione*, 1) speaks of the persistent requests and the party spirit of *advocates* (*paraklētoi*) serving the ends of private ambition instead of the public good. Diogenes Laertius, who wrote on the lives of the Greek philosophers (4:50), tells of a caustic saying of the philosopher Bion. A very talkative person sought his help in some matter. Bion said: 'I will do what you want, if you will only send someone to me to plead your case [that is, send a *paraklētos*], and stay away yourself.' When the Jewish scholar Philo is telling the story of Joseph and his brothers, he says that, when Joseph forgave them for the wrong that they had done him, he said: 'I offer you an amnesty for all that you did to me; you need no other *paraklētos*' (*Life of Joseph*, 40). Philo tells how the Jews of Alexandria were being oppressed by a certain governor and were determined to take their case to the emperor. 'We must find', they said, 'a more powerful *paraklētos* by whom the Emperor Gaius will be brought to a favourable disposition towards us' (*In Flaccum*, 968 B).

So common was this word that it came into other languages just as it stood. In the New Testament itself, the Syriac, Egyptian, Arabic and Ethiopic versions all keep the word *paraklētos* just as it stands. The Jews especially adopted the word and used it in this sense of *advocate*, someone to plead one's cause. They used it as the opposite of the word *accuser*, and the Rabbis had this saying about what would happen in the day of God's judgment. 'The man who keeps one commandment of the law has got to himself one *paraklētos*; the man who breaks one commandment of the law has got to himself one accuser.' They said: 'If a man is summoned to court on a capital charge, he needs powerful *paraklētoi* [the plural of the word] to save him; repentance and good works are his *paraklētoi* in the judgment of God.' 'All the righteousness and mercy which an Israelite does in this world are great peace and great *paraklētoi* between him and his father in heaven.' They said that the sin offering is a person's *paraklētos* before God.

So, the word came into the Christian vocabulary. In the days of the persecutions and the martyrs, a Christian called Vettius Epagathos ably pleaded the case of those who were accused of being Christians. 'He was an advocate [*paraklētos*] for the Christians, for he had the Advocate within himself, even the Spirit' (Eusebius, *Ecclesiastical History*, 5:1). The Letter of Barnabas (20) speaks of evil men who are the *advocates* of the wealthy and the unjust judges of the poor. The writer of 2 Clement asks: 'Who shall be your *paraklētos* if it be not clear that your works are righteous and holy?' (2 Clement 6:9).

A *paraklētos* has been defined as 'one who lends his presence to his friends'. More than once in the New Testament, there is this great conception of Jesus as the friend and the defender of men and women. In a military court-martial, the officer who defends the soldier under accusation is called the prisoner's friend. Jesus is our friend. Paul writes of that Christ who is at the right hand of God and 'who intercedes for us' (Romans 8:34). The writer of the Letter to

the Hebrews speaks of Jesus Christ as the one who 'always
lives to make intercession' (Hebrews 7:25); and he also speaks
of him as appearing 'in the presence of God on our behalf'
(Hebrews 9:24).

The tremendous thing about Jesus is that he has never lost
his interest in, or his love for, men and women. We are not to
think of him as having gone through his life upon the earth
and his death upon the cross, and then being finished with us.
He still bears his concern for us upon his heart; he still pleads
for us; Jesus Christ is the prisoner's friend for all.

JESUS CHRIST THE ATONING SACRIFICE

1 John 2:1−2 (*contd*)

JOHN goes on to say that Jesus is, as the Authorized Version
has it, *the propitiation for our sins*. The word is *hilasmos*.
This is a more difficult picture for us to grasp fully. The picture
of the *advocate* is universal, for we all have experience of a
friend coming to our aid; but the picture in *propitiation* is
less familiar. It comes from *sacrifice*; and, to understand it,
we must explore the basic ideas behind it.

The great aim of all religion is fellowship with God, to
know him as friend and to enter with joy, and not fear, into
his presence. It therefore follows that the supreme problem
of religion is sin, for it is sin that interrupts fellowship with
God. It is to meet that problem that all sacrifice arises. By
sacrifice, fellowship with God is restored. So, the Jews offered
– night and morning – the sin offering in the Temple. That
was the offering, not for any particular sin but for all people
as sinners; and, as long as the Temple lasted, it was made to
God in the morning and in the evening. The Jews also offered
their trespass offerings to God; these were the offerings for

particular sins. The Jews had their Day of Atonement, whose ritual was designed to atone for *all* sins, known and unknown. It is with that background that we must approach this picture of propitiation.

As we have said, the Greek word for *propitiation* is *hilasmos*; and the corresponding verb is *hilaskesthai*. This verb has three meanings. (1) When it is used with a person as the subject, it means *to placate* or *to pacify* someone who has been injured or offended, and especially to placate a god. It is to bring a sacrifice or to perform a ritual whereby a god, offended by sin, is pacified. (2) If the subject is *God*, the verb means *to forgive*, for then the meaning is that God himself provides the means whereby the lost relationship between him and the people concerned is restored. (3) The third meaning is allied with the first. The verb often means to perform some deed by which the taint of guilt is removed. People sin; at once they become tainted by sin; something is needed which, to use the scholar C. H. Dodd's metaphor, will *disinfect* them from that contamination and enable them once again to enter into the presence of God. In that sense, *hilaskesthai* means not to propitiate but to *expiate* – not so much to pacify God as to disinfect from the taint of sin and by that means make people once again fit to enter into fellowship with God.

When John says that Jesus is the *hilasmos* for our sins, he is, we think, bringing all these different meanings together into one. Jesus is the person through whom guilt for past sin and defilement from present sin are removed. The great basic truth behind this word is that it is through Jesus Christ that our fellowship with God is first restored and then maintained.

We note one other thing. As John sees it, this work of Jesus was carried out not only for us but for the whole world. There is in the New Testament a strong line of thought in which the universality of the salvation of God is stressed. God so loved *the world* that he sent his Son (John 3:16). Jesus is confident that, if he is lifted up, he will draw *all people* to him (John 12:32). God desires *everyone* to be saved (1 Timothy 2:4). It would indeed be a bold person who would set limits to the grace and love of God or to the effectiveness of the work and sacrifice of Jesus Christ. Truly, as F. W. Faber's hymn has it, 'the love of God is broader than the measures of man's mind'; and in the New Testament itself there are hints of a salvation whose arms are as wide as the world.

THE TRUE KNOWLEDGE OF GOD

1 John 2:3–6

> And it is by this that we know that we have come to know him – if we keep his commandments. He who says: 'I have come to know him' and who does not keep his commandments is a liar, and the truth is not in such a man. The love of God is truly perfected in any man who keeps his word. This is the way in which we know that we are in him. He who claims that he abides in him ought himself to live the same kind of life as he lived.

THIS passage deals in phrases and thoughts which were very familiar in the ancient world. People talked a good deal about *knowing God* and about *being in God*. It is important that we should see where the differences lay between the Gentile world in all its greatness and Judaism and Christianity. To know God, to abide in God and to have fellowship with God has always been the quest of the human spirit, for St Augustine was right when he said that God had made us for himself and that our hearts were restless until they found their rest in him. We may say that, in the ancient world, there were three lines of thought in regard to knowing God.

(1) In the great classical age of their thought and literature, in the sixth and fifth centuries before Christ, the Greeks were convinced that they could arrive at God by the sheer process of intellectual reasoning and argument. In *The World of the New Testament*, T. R. Glover has a chapter on 'The Greek' in which he brilliantly and vividly sketches the character of the Greek mind in its greatest days when the Greeks glorified the intellect. 'A harder and more precise thinker than Plato it will be difficult to discover,' said the classicist, Marshall Macgregor. The Greek historian Xenophon tells of a conversation Socrates had with a young man. 'How do you know that?' asked Socrates. 'Do you know it or are you guessing?' The young man had to say: 'I am guessing.' 'Very well,' answered Socrates, 'when we are done with guessing and when we know, shall we talk about it then?' Guesses were not good enough for the Greek thinkers.

To the classical Greeks, curiosity was not a fault but was the greatest of the virtues, for it was the mother of philosophy. Glover writes of this outlook: 'Everything must be examined; all the world is the proper study of man; there is no question which it is wrong for man to ask; nature in the long run must stand and deliver; God too must explain himself, for did he not make man so?' For the Greeks of the great classical age, the way to God was by means of the intellect.

It has to be noted that an intellectual approach to religion is not necessarily ethical at all. If religion is a series of mental problems, if God is the goal at the end of intense mental activity, religion becomes something not very unlike higher mathematics. It becomes intellectual satisfaction and not moral action; and the plain fact is that many of the great

Greek thinkers were not especially good individuals. It was possible to know God in the intellectual sense; but that did not necessarily make people good.

(2) The later Greeks, in the period which was the immediate background to the New Testament, sought to find God in emotional experience. The characteristic religious phenomenon of these days was the mystery religions. In any view of the history of religion, they are an amazing feature. Their aim was union with the divine, and they were all in the form of passion plays. They were all founded on the story of some god who lived, and suffered terribly, and died a cruel death, and rose again. The initiate was given a long course of instruction; he was made to practise a discipline of self-denial. He was worked up to an intense pitch of expectation and emotional sensitivity. He was then allowed to come to a passion play in which the story of the suffering, dying and rising god was played out on the stage. Everything was designed to heighten the emotional atmosphere. There was cunning lighting, sensuous music, perfumed incense and a marvellous liturgy. In this atmosphere, the story was played out and the worshipper identified himself with the experiences of the god until he could cry out: 'I am thou, and thou art I'; until he shared the god's suffering and also shared his victory and immortality.

This was not so much *knowing* God as *feeling* God. But it was a highly emotional experience and, as such, it was necessarily of the moment. It was a kind of religious drug. It quite definitely found God in an abnormal experience, and its aim was to escape from ordinary life.

(3) Last, there was the Jewish way of knowing God which is closely allied with the Christian way. To the Jews, knowledge of God came not by human speculation or by an exotic experience of emotion but by God's own revelation.

God who revealed himself was a holy God, and his ~ess~ brought the obligation to every worshipper to be holy too. In his commentary on the Johannine Epistles, A. E. Brooke says: 'John can conceive of no real knowledge of God which does not issue in obedience.' Knowledge of God can be proved only by obedience to God; and knowledge of God can be gained only by obedience to God. The biblical scholar C. H. Dodd says: 'To know God is to experience his love in Christ, and to return that love in obedience.'

Here was John's problem. In the Greek world, he was faced with people who saw God as part of an intellectual exercise and who could say 'I know God' without being conscious of any ethical obligation whatever. In the Greek world, he was faced with people who had had an emotional experience and who could say: 'I am in God and God is in me,' and yet who did not see God in terms of commandments at all.

John is determined to lay it down quite unmistakably and without compromise that the only way in which we can show that we know God is by obedience to him, and the only way we can show that we have union with Christ is by imitation of him. Christianity is the religion which offers the greatest privilege and brings with it the greatest obligation. Intellectual effort and emotional experience are not neglected – far from it – but they must combine to produce moral action.

THE COMMANDMENT WHICH IS OLD AND NEW

1 John 2:7–8

> Beloved, it is not a new commandment which I am writing to you, but an old commandment which you had from the beginning; the old commandment is the word which you heard. Again, it is a new commandment

which I am writing to you, a thing which is true in him
and in you, because the darkness is passing away and
the light is now shining.

JOHN's favourite address to his people is *Beloved* (cf. 3:2,
3:21, 4:1, 4:7; 3 John 1, 2, 5, 11). The whole accent of his
writing is love. As the New Testament scholar B. F. Westcott
puts it, 'St John, while enforcing the commandment of love,
gives expression to it.' There is something very lovely here.
So much of this letter is a warning; and parts of it are a rebuke.
When we are warning people or rebuking them, it is so
easy to become coldly critical; it is so easy to scold; it is even
possible to take a cruel pleasure in seeing people wince under
the sharpness of our tongues. But, even when he has to say
hard things, the accent of John's voice is love. He had learned
the lesson which every parent, every preacher, every teacher,
every leader must learn: he had learned to speak the truth in
love.

John speaks about a commandment which is at one and
the same time old and new. Some would take this as referring
to the implied commandment in verse 6 that those who abide
in Jesus Christ must live the same kind of life as their Master
lived. But, almost certainly, John is thinking of the words of
Jesus in the Fourth Gospel: 'I give you a new commandment, that you love one another. Just as I have loved you,
you also should love one another' (John 13:34). In what sense
was that commandment both old and new?

(1) It was old in the sense that it was already there in the
Old Testament. Did not the law say: 'You shall love your
neighbour as yourself' (Leviticus 19:18)? It was old in the
sense that this was not the first time that John's hearers had
heard it. From the very first day of their entry into the
Christian life, they had been taught that the law of love must

be the law of their lives. This commandment went a long way back in history and a long way back in the lives of those to whom John was speaking.

(2) It was new in that it had been raised to a completely new standard in the life of Jesus – and it was as Jesus had loved them that they were now to love each other. It could well be said that people did not really know what love was until they saw it in him. In every sphere of life, it is possible for a thing to be old in the sense that it has been in existence for a long time, and yet to reach a completely new standard in someone's performance of it. A game may become a new game for us when we have seen some expert play it. A piece of music may become new to us when we hear some great orchestra play it under the baton of an inspirational conductor. Even a dish of food can become a new experience for us when we taste it after it has been prepared by someone with a genius for cooking. An old thing can become a new experience in the hands of someone with the right touch. In Jesus, love became new in two directions.

(a) It became new in *the extent to which it reached*. In Jesus, love reached out *to the sinner*. To the orthodox Jewish Rabbi, the sinner was a person whom God wished to destroy. 'There is joy in heaven', they said, 'when one sinner is obliterated from the earth.' But Jesus was the friend of outcast men and women and of sinners, and he was sure that there was joy in heaven when one sinner came home. In Jesus, love reached out *to the Gentiles*. As the Rabbis saw it, 'The Gentiles were created by God to be fuel for the fires of Hell.' But, in Jesus, God so loved *the world* that he gave his Son. Love became new in Jesus because he widened its boundaries until no one was outside its embrace.

(b) It became new in *the lengths to which it would go*. No lack of response, nothing that anyone could ever do to him, could turn Jesus' love to hate. He could even pray for God's mercy on those who were nailing him to his cross.

The commandment to love was old in the sense that it had been known for a long time; but it was new because, in Jesus Christ, love had reached a standard which it had never reached before, and it was by that standard that men and women were commanded to love.

THE DEFEAT OF THE DARK

1 John 2:7–8 (*contd*)

JOHN goes on to say that this commandment of love is true in Jesus Christ and true in the people to whom he is writing. To John, as we have seen, truth was not only something to be grasped with the mind; it was something to be done. What he means is that the commandment to love one another is the highest truth; in Jesus Christ, we can see that commandment in all the glory of its fullness; in him, that commandment is true; and in Christians we can see it, not in the fullness of its truth, but coming true. For John, Christianity is progress in love.

He goes on to say that the light is shining and the darkness is passing away. This must be read in context. By the time John wrote, at the end of the first century, ideas were changing. In the very early days, people had looked for the second coming of Jesus as a sudden and shattering event within their own lifetime. When that did not happen, they did not abandon the hope but allowed experience to change it. To John, the second coming of Christ is not one sudden, dramatic event but a process in which the darkness is steadily being defeated by the light; and the end of the process will be a world in which the darkness is totally defeated and the light triumphant.

In this passage, and in verses 10–11, the light is identified with love and the dark with hate. That is to say, the end of this process is a world where love reigns supreme and hate is banished forever. Christ has entered the individual heart when a person's whole being is ruled by love; and he will have come in the world when all men and women obey his commandment of love. The coming and reign of Jesus is identical with the coming and reign of love.

LOVE AND HATE, LIGHT AND DARK

I John 2:9–11

> He who says that he is in the light, and who at the same time hates his brother, is still in the darkness. He who loves his brother abides in the light, and there is nothing in him which makes him stumble. He who hates his brother is in the darkness and he is walking in darkness, and he does not know where he is going, because the darkness has blinded his eyes.

THE first thing which strikes us about this passage is the way in which John sees personal relationships in terms of black and white. When it comes to our neighbours, it is a case of either love or hate; as John sees it, there is no such thing as neutrality in personal relationships. As Westcott put it, 'Indifference is impossible; there is no twilight in the spiritual world.'

It is further to be noted that what John is speaking about is our attitude to our *brothers and sisters*, that is, to the people next door, those beside whom we live and work, the people with whom we come into contact every day. There is a kind of Christian attitude which enthusiastically preaches love to the world but has never sought any kind of fellowship with its next-door neighbour or even managed to live at peace within its own family circle. John insists on love for the people with whom we are in daily contact. As the commentator A. E. Brooke puts it, this is not 'vapid philosophy, or a pretentious cosmopolitanism'; it is immediate and practical.

John was perfectly right when he drew his sharp distinction between light and dark, and love and hate, without shades and half-way stages. Our neighbours cannot be disregarded; they are part of the landscape. The question is: *how* do we regard them?

(1) We may regard other people as *negligible*. We can make all our plans without taking them into our calculations at all. We can live on the assumption that their need and their sorrow, their welfare and their salvation have nothing to do with us. It is possible to be so self-centred – often quite unconsciously – that in our world no one matters except us.

(2) We may regard other people with *contempt*. We may treat them as fools in comparison with our intellectual attainment and as people whose opinions are to be brushed aside. We may regard them much as the Greeks regarded slaves – inferior, useful enough in their way, but not a patch on us.

(3) We may regard other people as a *nuisance*. We may feel that law and convention have given them a certain claim upon us, but that claim is nothing more than an unfortunate necessity. Thus we may regard any gift we have to make to charity and any tax we have to pay for social welfare as regrettable. Some people, in their heart of hearts, regard those who find themselves in poverty or in sickness and those who are underprivileged as mere nuisances.

(4) We may regard other people as *enemies*. If we regard competition as the principle of life, that is bound to be the

case. Everyone else in the same profession or trade is a potential competitor and, therefore, a potential enemy.

(5) We may regard other people as *brothers and sisters*. We may regard their needs as our needs, their interests as our interests, and to be in fellowship with them as the true joy of life.

THE EFFECT OF LOVE AND HATE

1 John 2:9–11 (*contd*)

JOHN has something further to say. As he sees it, our attitude to other people has an effect not only on them but also on ourselves.

(1) If we love others, we are walking in the light, and there is nothing in us which causes us to stumble. The Greek could mean that, if we love others, there is nothing in us which causes *them* to stumble – and, of course, that would be perfectly true. But it is much more likely that John is saying that, if we love other people, there is nothing in us which causes *us* to stumble. That is to say, love enables us to make progress in the spiritual life, and hatred makes progress impossible. When we think of it, that is perfectly obvious. If God is love and if the new commandment of Christ is love, then love brings us nearer to one another and to God, and hatred separates us from one another and from God. We ought always to remember that those who have in their hearts hatred, resentment and the unforgiving spirit can never grow up in the spiritual life.

(2) John goes on to say that those who hate other people walk in darkness and do not know where they are going, because the darkness has blinded them. That is to say, hatred makes us blind – and this, too, is perfectly obvious. When people have hatred in their hearts, their powers of judgment

are obscured; they cannot see an issue clearly. It is not uncommon to see people opposing a good proposal simply because they dislike, or have quarrelled with, the person who made it. Again and again, progress in some plans for a church or a group is held up because of personal animosities. No one who has a heart filled with hatred is fit to give a verdict on anything, and being dominated by hatred prevents people from finding a right direction in life.

Love enables us to walk in the light; hatred leaves us in the dark, even if we do not realize that it is so.

REMEMBERING WHO WE ARE

1 John 2:12–14

> I am writing to you, little children,
>> Because your sins are forgiven you through his name.
> I am writing to you, fathers,
>> Because you have come to know him who is from the beginning.
> I am writing to you, young men,
>> Because you have overcome the evil one.
> I have written to you, little ones,
>> Because you have come to know the Father.
> I have written to you, fathers,
>> Because you have come to know him who is from the beginning.
> I have written to you, young men,
>> Because you are strong,
>> And the word of God abides in you,
>> And you have overcome the evil one.

THIS is a very lovely passage – and yet, for all its beauty, it has its problems of interpretation. We may begin by noting two things which are certain.

First, as to its form, this passage is not exactly poetry; but it is certainly poetical and strongly rhythmical. Therefore, it is to be interpreted as poetry ought to be.

Second, as to its contents, John has been warning his people of the perils of the dark and the necessity of walking in the light, and now he says that in every case their best defence is to remember what they are and what has been done for them. No matter who they are, their sins have been forgiven; no matter who they are, they know the one who is from the beginning; no matter who they are, they have the strength which can face and overcome the evil one. When Nehemiah was urged to seek a cowardly safety, his answer was: 'Should a man like me run away?' (Nehemiah 6:11). And when Christians are tempted, their answer may well be: 'Should someone like me stoop to this folly or stain my hands with this evil?' People who are forgiven, who know God and who are aware that they can draw on a strength beyond their own, have a great defence against temptation in simply remembering these things.

But, in this passage, there are problems. The first is quite simple. Why does John say three times *I am writing* and three times *I have written*? The Latin version of the Bible, the Vulgate, translates both by the present tense *scribo*; and it has been argued that John varies the tense simply to avoid the monotony that six successive present tenses would bring. It has also been argued that the past tenses are what Greek calls the *epistolary aorist*. Greek letter-writers had a habit of using the past instead of the present tense because they put themselves in the position of the reader. To the *writer* of a letter, a thing may be *present* because at that moment it is a *present* activity; but, to the *reader* of the letter, it will be *past* because by that time it has been done. To take a simple instance, a Greek letter-writer might equally well say: 'I am going to town today,' or: 'I went to town today.' That is the Greek *epistolary* or *letter-writer's aorist*. If that is the case here, there is no real difference between John's *I am writing* and *I have written*.

A more likely explanation is this. When John says *I am writing*, he is thinking of what he is at the moment writing and of what he still has to say; when he says *I have written*, he is thinking of what has already been written and his readers have already read. The sense would then be that the whole letter – the part already written, the part being written and the part still to come – is all designed to remind Christians of who and whose they are and of what has been done for them.

For John, it was of supreme importance that Christians should remember the status and the benefits they have in Jesus Christ, for these would be their defence against error and against sin.

AT EVERY STAGE

1 John 2:12–14 (*contd*)

THE second problem which confronts us is more difficult and also more important. John uses three titles of the people to whom he is writing. He calls them *little children*. In verse 12, the Greek word is *teknia*, and in verse 13 *paidia*; *teknia* indicates a child young in age, and *paidia* a child young in experience and, therefore, in need of training and discipline. He calls them *fathers*. He calls them *young men*. The question then is: to whom is John writing? Three answers have been given.

(1) It is suggested that we are to take these words as representing three age groups in the Church – children, fathers and young men. The *children* have the sweet innocence of

childhood and of forgiveness. The *fathers* have the mature wisdom which Christian experience can bring. The *young* people have the strength which enables them to win their personal battle with the evil one. That is most attractive; but there are three reasons which make us hesitate to adopt it as the only meaning of the passage.

(a) *Little children* is one of John's favourite expressions. He also uses it in 2:1, 2:28, 3:7, 4:4 and 5:21; and it is clear in the other cases that he is thinking not of *little children* in terms of age but of Christians whose spiritual father he is. By this time, he must have been very nearly 100 years old; all the members of his churches were of a far younger generation, and to him they were all little children in the same way as teachers or professors may still think of their boys and girls after the boys and girls have long since become men and women.

(b) The fact that the passage is very like poetry makes us think twice before insisting that so literal a meaning must be given to the words and so cut and dried a classification be taken as intended. Literalism and poetry do not go comfortably hand in hand.

(c) Perhaps the greatest difficulty is that the blessings of which John speaks are not the exclusive possession of any one age group. Forgiveness does not belong to the child alone; a Christian may be young in the faith, and yet have a wonderful maturity; strength to overcome the tempter does not – thank God – belong to youth alone. These blessings are the blessings not of any one age group but of the Christian life.

We do not say that there is no thought of age groups in this. There almost certainly is; but John has a way of saying things which can be taken in two ways, a narrower and a wider; and, while the narrower meaning is here, we must go beyond it to find the full meaning.

(2) It is suggested that we are to find two groups here. The argument is that *little children* describes *Christians in general* and that Christians in general are then divided into two groups, the fathers and the young people – that is, the young and the old, the mature and the as yet immature. That is perfectly possible, because John's people must have become so used to hearing him call them *my little children* that they would not connect the words with age at all but would always include themselves in that form of address.

(3) It is suggested that, in every case, the words include *all* Christians and that no classification is intended. *All* Christians are like little children, for all can regain their innocence by the forgiveness of Jesus Christ. *All* Christians are like fathers, like full-grown, responsible adults, who can think and learn their way deeper and deeper into the knowledge of Jesus Christ. *All* Christians are like young people, with a vigorous strength to fight and win their battles against the tempter and his power. It seems to us that indeed this is John's wider meaning. We may begin by taking his words as a classification of Christians into three age groups; but we come to see that the blessings of each group are the blessings of all the groups and that we can all find ourselves included in all of them.

GOD'S GIFTS IN CHRIST

1 John 2:12–14 (*contd*)

THIS passage sets out God's gifts to all people in Jesus Christ.

(1) There is the gift of *forgiveness through Jesus Christ*. This was the essential message of the gospel and of the early preachers. They were sent out to preach repentance and

forgiveness of sins (Luke 24:47). It was Paul's message at Antioch in Pisidia that to all people forgiveness of sins was proclaimed through Jesus Christ (Acts 13:38). To be forgiven is to be at peace with God – and that is precisely the gift that Jesus brought to men and women.

John uses the curious phrase *through his name* (verse 12). Forgiveness comes *through the name* of Jesus Christ. The Jews used *the name* in a very special way. The name is not simply what a person is called; it stands for the whole character of a person in so far as it has been made known to others. This use is very common in the Book of Psalms. 'And those who know your name put their trust in you' (Psalm 9:10). This clearly does not mean that those who know that God is called *Yahweh* will put their trust in him; it means that those who know God's nature in so far as it has been revealed will be ready to put their trust in him, because they know what he is like. The psalmist prays: 'For your name's sake, O Lord, pardon my guilt' (Psalm 25:11), which to all intents and purposes means *for your love and mercy's sake*. The grounds of the psalmist's prayer are the character of God as it is known. 'For your name's sake', prays the psalmist, 'lead me and guide me' (Psalm 31:3). The request can be brought only because the psalmist knows the name – the character – of God. 'Some take pride in chariots,' says the psalmist, 'and some in horses; but our pride is in the name of the Lord our God' (Psalm 20:7). Some people put their trust in earthly help; but we will trust God, because we know his nature.

So, John means that we are assured of forgiveness because we know the character of Jesus Christ. We know that in him we see God. We see in him sacrificial love and patient mercy; therefore we know that God is like that; and, therefore, we can be sure that there is forgiveness for us.

(2) There is the gift of *increasing knowledge of God*. John was no doubt thinking of his own experience. He was an old man now; he was writing about AD 100. For seventy years, he had lived with Christ and had thought about him and come to know him better every day. For the Jews, knowledge was not merely an intellectual thing. To know God was not merely to know him as the philosopher knows him; it was to know him as a friend knows him. In Hebrew, *to know* is used of the relationship between husband and wife and especially of the sexual act, the most intimate of all relationships (cf. Genesis 4:1). When John spoke of the increasing knowledge of God, he did not mean that, as time went on, Christians would become more learned theologians; he meant that, throughout the years, they would become more and more intimately friendly with God.

(3) There is the *gift of victorious strength*. John looks on the struggle with temptation as a personal struggle. He does not speak in the abstract of conquering evil; he speaks of conquering the evil one. He sees evil as a personal power which seeks to seduce us from God. Once, the writer Robert Louis Stevenson, speaking of an experience which he never talked about in detail, said: 'You know the Caledonian Railway Station in Edinburgh? *Once I met Satan there*.' Every one of us, at some time or other, must have experienced the attack of the tempter, the personal assault on our virtue and on our loyalty. It is in Christ that we receive the power to meet and to defeat that attack. To take a very simple human analogy: we all know that there are some people in whose presence it is easy to be bad and some in whose presence it is possible only to be good. When we walk with Jesus, we are walking with the one whose company can enable us to defeat the assaults of the evil one.

RIVALS FOR THE HUMAN HEART

1 John 2:15–17

> Do not love the world nor the things in the world. If
> anyone loves the world, the love of the Father is not in
> him. For everything that is in the world – the flesh's
> desire, the eye's desire, life's empty pride – does not
> come from the Father but comes from the world. And
> the world is passing away, and so is its desire; but he
> who does God's will abides forever.

IT was characteristic of ancient thought to see the world in
terms of two conflicting principles. We see this very vividly
in Zoroastrianism, the religion of the Persians. That was a
religion with which the Jews had been brought into contact
and which had left a mark upon their thinking. Zoroastrianism
saw the world as the battle ground between the opposing
forces of the light and the dark. The god of the light was
Ahura-Mazda, the god of the dark was Angra-Mainyu; and
the great decision in life was which side to serve. Every
individual had to decide whether to side with the light or
with the dark; that was a conception which the Jews were
familiar with.

But, for Christians, the split between the world and the
Church had another background. The Jews had for many
centuries held to a basic belief which divided time into two
ages – *this present age*, which was wholly evil, and *the age
to come*, which was the age of God and, therefore, wholly
good. It was a basic belief of Christians that in Christ the age
to come had arrived; the kingdom of God was here. But the
kingdom of God had not arrived in and for the *world*; it had
arrived only in and for the *Church*. Hence Christians were
bound to draw a contrast. The life of Christians within the

Church was the life of the age to come, which was wholly good. On the other hand, the world was still living in the present age, which was wholly evil. It followed inevitably that there was a complete split between the Church and the world, and that there could be no fellowship, and even no compromise, between them.

But we must be careful to understand what John meant by the world, the *kosmos*. Christians did not hate *the world as such*. It was God's creation; and God made all things well. Jesus had loved the beauty of the world; not even Solomon in all his glory was clothed like one of the scarlet anemones which bloomed for a day and died. Jesus again and again took his illustrations from the world. In that sense, Christians did not hate the world. The earth was not the devil's; the earth and all its fullness was the Lord's. But *kosmos* acquired a moral sense. It began to mean *the world apart from God*. C. H. Dodd defines this meaning of *kosmos*: 'Our author means human society in so far as it is organized on wrong principles, and characterized by base desires, false values, and egoism.' In other words, to John *the world was nothing other than the society of the Roman Empire* with its false values and its false gods.

The world in this passage does not mean the world in general, for God loved the world which he had made; it means the world which, in fact, had forsaken the God who made it.

It so happened that there was a factor in the situation of John's people which made the circumstances even more perilous. It is clear that, although they might be unpopular, they were not undergoing persecution. They were, therefore, under the great and dangerous temptation to compromise with the world. It is always difficult to be different, and it was particularly difficult for them.

To this day, Christians cannot escape the obligation to be different from the world. In this passage, John sees things as he always sees them – in terms of black and white. As B. F. Westcott has it, 'There cannot be a vacuum in the soul.' This is a matter in which there is no neutrality; a person loves either the world or God. Jesus himself said: 'No one can serve two masters' (Matthew 6:24). The ultimate choice remains the same. Are we to accept the world's standards or the standards of God?

THE LIFE IN WHICH THERE IS NO FUTURE

1 John 2:15–17 (contd)

JOHN has two things to say about those who love the world and who compromise with it. First, he sets out three sins which are typical of the world.

(1) There is the *flesh's desire*. This means far more than what we mean by *sins of the flesh*. To us, that expression has to do exclusively with sexual sin. But, in the New Testament, *the flesh* is that part of our nature which, when it is without the grace of Jesus Christ, offers a point of entry for sin. It includes the sins of the flesh but also all worldly ambitions and selfish aims. To be subject to physical desire is to judge everything in this world by purely material standards. It is to live a life dominated by the senses. It is to be gluttonous in eating habits, soft in luxury, slavish in pleasure, lustful and lax in morals, selfish in the use of possessions, heedless of all the spiritual values and extravagant in the gratification of material desires. The flesh's desire is heedless of the commandments of God, the judgment of God, the standards of God and the very existence of God. We need not think of this as the sin of the gross sinner. Anyone who demands a pleasure

which may be the ruin of someone else, anyone who has no respect for the personalities of other people in the gratification of personal desires, anyone who lives in luxury while others live in want, anyone who has made a god of comfort and of ambition in any part of life, is the servant of physical desire.

(2) There is the *eye's desire*. This, as C. H. Dodd puts it, is 'the tendency to be captivated by outward show'. It is the spirit which identifies lavish ostentation with real prosperity. It is the spirit which can see nothing without wishing to acquire it and which, having acquired it, flaunts it. It is the spirit which believes that happiness is to be found in the things that money can buy and the eye can see; it has no values other than the material.

(3) There is *life's empty pride*. Here, John uses a most vivid Greek word, *alazoneia*. To the ancient moralists, the *alazōn* was the man who laid claims to possessions and to achievements which did not belong to him in order to exalt himself. The *alazōn* is the braggart; and C. H. Dodd translates *alazoneia* as *pretentious egoism*. Theophrastus, the great Greek master of the character study, has a study of the *alazōn*. He stands in the harbour and boasts of the ships that he has at sea; he ostentatiously sends a messenger to the bank when he has very little to his credit; he talks of his friends among the mighty and of the letters he receives from the famous. He details at length his charitable donations and his services to the state. He only lives in rented accommodation, but he talks of buying a bigger house to match his lavish entertaining. His conversation is a continual boasting about things which he does not possess, and all his life is spent in an attempt to impress everyone he meets with his own non-existent importance.

As John sees them, the men and women of the world are people who judge everything by their own appetites, the slaves of lavish ostentation, boastful braggarts who try to make themselves out to be far more important than they really are.

Then comes John's second warning. Those who attach themselves to the world's aims and the world's ways are giving their lives to things which literally have no future. All these things are passing away, and none of them has any permanency. But those who have taken God as the centre of their lives have given themselves to the things which last forever. The people of this world are doomed to disappointment; the people of God are assured of lasting joy.

THE TIME OF THE LAST HOUR

1 John 2:18

> Little children, it is the time of the last hour; and now many antichrists have risen, just as you heard that antichrist was to come. That is how we know that it is the time of the last hour.

IT is important that we should understand what John means when he speaks of the time of the last hour. The idea of the last days and of the last hour runs all through the Bible; but there is a most interesting development in its meaning.

(1) The phrase occurs frequently in the very early books of the Old Testament. Jacob, for instance, before his death assembles his sons to tell them what will happen to them in the last days (Genesis 49:1; cf. Numbers 24:14). At that time, the last days were when the people of Israel would enter into the promised land and would at last enter into full enjoyment of the promised blessings of God.

(2) The phrase frequently occurs in the prophets. In the last days, the mountain of the Lord shall be established as

the highest of the mountains, and shall be raised above the hills, and all nations shall stream to it (Isaiah 2:2; Micah 4:1). In the last days, God's holy city will be supreme; and Israel will render to God the perfect obedience which is his due (cf. Jeremiah 23:20, 30:24, 48:47). In the last days, there will be the supremacy of God and the obedience of his people.

(3) In the Old Testament itself, and in the times between the Old and the New Testaments, the last days become associated with the day of the Lord. No conception is more deeply interwoven into Scripture than this. The Jews had come to believe that all time was divided into two ages. In between *this present age*, which was wholly evil, and *the age to come*, which was the golden time of God's supremacy, there was the day of the Lord, the last days, which would be a time of terror, of cosmic disintegration and destruction, and of judgment – the birth-pangs of the new age.

The last hour does not mean a time of annihilation whose end will be a great nothingness as there was at the beginning. In biblical thought, the last time is the end of one age and the beginning of another. It is *last* in the sense that things as they are pass away; but it leads not to world obliteration but to world re-creation.

Here is the heart of the matter. The question then becomes: 'Will people be wiped out in the judgment of the old, or will they enter into the glory of the new?' That is the alternative with which John – like all the biblical writers – is confronting men and women. They have the choice of allying themselves with the old world, which is doomed to dissolution, or of allying themselves with Christ and entering into the new world, the very world of God. Here lies the urgency. If it was a simple matter of utter obliteration, no one could do anything about it. But it is a matter of re-creation; and whether people will enter the new world or not depends on whether or not they give their lives to Jesus Christ.

In fact, John was wrong. It was not the last hour for his people – for 1,900 years have gone by, and the world still exists. Does the whole conception, then, belong to a sphere of thought which must be discarded? The answer is that in this conception there is an eternal relevance. *Every hour is the last hour.* In the world, there is a continual conflict between good and evil, between God and that which is anti-God. And, in every moment and in every decision, we are confronted with the choice of allying ourselves either with God or with the evil forces which are against God, and of thereby ensuring, or failing to ensure, our own share in eternal life. The conflict between good and evil never stops; therefore, the choice never stops; therefore, in a very real sense, every hour is the last hour.

THE ANTICHRIST

1 John 2:18 (*contd*)

IN this verse, we meet the conception of *antichrist. Antichrist* is a word which occurs in the New Testament only in John's letters (1 John 2:22, 4:3; 2 John 7); but it is the expression of an idea which is as old as religion itself.

From its derivation, *antichrist* can have two meanings. *Anti* is a Greek preposition which can mean either *against* or *in place of. Stratēgos* is the Greek word for a *commander*, and *antistratēgos* can mean either the *hostile commander* or the *deputy commander. Antichrist* can mean either the opponent of Christ or the one who seeks to put himself in the place of Christ. In this case, the meaning will come to the same thing – but with this difference. If we take the meaning to be *the one who is opposed to Christ*, the opposition is plain. If we take the meaning to be *the one who seeks to put himself in the place of Christ*, antichrist can be one who subtly tries to take the place of Christ from within the Church and the Christian community. The one will be an open opposition, the other a subtle infiltration. We need not choose between these meanings, for antichrist can act in either way.

The simplest way to think of it is that Christ is the incarnation of God and goodness, and antichrist is the incarnation of the devil and evil.

We began by saying that this is an idea which is as old as religion itself; people have always felt that in the universe there is a power which is in opposition to God. One of its earliest forms occurs in the Babylonian legend of creation. According to it, there was in the very beginning a primeval sea monster called Tiamat; this sea monster was subdued by Marduk but not killed; it was only asleep, and the final battle was still to come. That mythical idea of the primeval monster occurs in the Old Testament again and again. There, the monster is often called Rahab, or the crooked serpent, or leviathan. 'You crushed Rahab like a carcass,' says the psalmist (Psalm 89:10). 'His hand pierced the fleeing serpent,' says Job (Job 26:13). Isaiah, speaking of the arm of the Lord, says: 'Was it not you who cut Rahab in pieces, who pierced the dragon?' (Isaiah 51:9). Isaiah writes: 'On that day the Lord with his cruel and great and strong sword will punish Leviathan the fleeing serpent, Leviathan the twisting serpent, and he will kill the dragon that is in the sea' (Isaiah 27:1). All these are references to the primeval dragon. This idea is obviously one which belongs to the childhood of humanity, and its basis is that in the universe there is a power hostile to God.

Originally, this power was conceived of as the dragon. Inevitably, as time went on, it became personalized. Every time there arose a very evil man who seemed to be setting himself against God and intent on the obliteration of his people, the tendency was to identify him with this anti-God force. For instance, about 168 BC there emerged the figure of Antiochus Epiphanes, king of Syria. He resolved on a deliberate attempt to eliminate Judaism from this earth. He invaded Jerusalem, killed thousands of Jews, and sold tens of thousands into slavery. To circumcise a child or to own a copy of the law was made a crime punishable by instant death. A great altar to Zeus was erected in the Temple courts. Pig's flesh was offered on it. The Temple chambers were made into public brothels. Here was a cold-blooded effort to wipe out the Jewish religion. It was Antiochus whom Daniel called 'the abomination that desolates' (Daniel 11:31; 12:11). Here, people thought, was the anti-God force in human form.

It was this same phrase that was used in the days of Mark's gospel when people talked of what the Authorized Version calls 'The Abomination of Desolation' – 'The Appalling Horror', as James Moffatt translates it – being set up in the Temple (Mark 13:14; Matthew 24:15). Here, the reference was to Caligula, the more than half-mad Roman emperor, who wanted to set up his own image in the Holy of Holies in the Temple. It was felt that this was the act of anti-God incarnate.

In 2 Thessalonians 2:3–4, Paul speaks of 'the lawless one', the one who exalts himself above all that is called God and all that is worshipped and who sets himself up in the very Temple of God. We do not know whom Paul was expecting, but again there is this thought of one who was the incarnation of everything which was opposed to God.

In Revelation, there is the beast (13:1, 16:13, 19:20, 20:10). Here is very probably another figure. Nero was regarded by all as a human monster. His excesses disgusted the Romans, and his savage persecution tortured the Christians. In due time, he died; but he had been so wicked that people could not believe that he was really dead. And so there arose the *Nero Redivivus* – Nero resurrected – legend, which said that Nero was not dead but had gone to Parthia and would come with the Parthian forces to descend upon the people. He is the beast, the antichrist, the incarnation of evil.

All through history, there have been these identifications of human figures with antichrist. Napoleon, Mussolini and Hitler have all in their day received this identification.

But the fact is that antichrist is not so much a person as a principle, the principle which is actively opposed to God and which may well be thought of as incarnating itself in those in every generation who have seemed to be the blatant opponents of God.

THE BATTLE OF THE MIND

1 John 2:18 (*contd*)

JOHN has a view of antichrist which is characteristically his own. To him, the sign that antichrist is in the world is the false belief and the dangerous teaching of the heretics. The Church had been well forewarned that in the last days false teachers would come. Jesus had said: 'Many will come in my name and say, "I am he!" and they will lead many astray' (Mark 13:6; cf. Matthew 24:5). Before he left them, Paul had warned his Ephesian friends: 'After I have gone, savage wolves will come in among you, not sparing the flock. Some even from your own group will come distorting the truth in order to entice the disciples to follow them' (Acts 20:29–30). The situation which had been foretold had now arisen.

But John had a special view of this situation. He did not think of antichrist as one single individual figure but rather as a power of falsehood speaking in and through the false teachers. Just as the Holy Spirit was inspiring the true teachers and the true prophets, so there was an evil spirit inspiring the false teachers and the false prophets.

The great interest and relevance of this is that, for John, *the battle ground was in the mind*. The spirit of antichrist was struggling with the Spirit of God for the possession of human minds. What makes this so significant is that we can see exactly this process at work today. Some people have made a science out of the indoctrination of the human mind. We see them take an idea and repeat it and repeat it until it settles into the minds of others who begin to accept it as true simply because they have heard it so often. This is easier today than it ever was with so many means of mass communication – books, newspapers, radio, television and the vast resources of modern advertising. A skilled propagandist can take an idea and infiltrate it into people's minds until, unknown to themselves, they are indoctrinated with it. We do not say that John foresaw all this, but he did see the mind as the field of operations for antichrist. He thought no longer in terms of a single demonic figure but in terms of a force of evil deliberately seeking to pervade people's minds; and there is nothing more potent for evil than that.

If there is one special task which confronts the Church today, it is to learn how to use the power of the media of mass communication to counteract the evil ideas with which the minds of men and women are being deliberately indoctrinated.

THE SIFTING OF THE CHURCH

1 John 2:19–21

> They have gone out from among us but they are not of
> our number. If they had been of our number, they would
> have remained with us. But things have happened as
> they have happened, that it may be clearly demonstrated
> that all of them are not of us. But you have received
> anointing from the Holy One and you all possess
> knowledge. I have not written this letter to you because
> you do not know the truth, but because you do know it
> and because no lie comes from the truth.

As things have turned out, John sees in the Church a time of
sifting. The false teachers had voluntarily left the Christian
fellowship; and that fact had shown that they did not really
belong there. They did not belong, and their own conduct
had shown that to be the case.

The last phrase of verse 19 can have two meanings.

(1) It may mean, as in our translation, 'All of them are
not of us' – or, as we might put it rather better, 'None of
them is from us.' That is to say, however attractive some
of them may be and however fine their teaching sounds,
all of them are alien to the Church.

(2) It is just possible that what the phrase means is that
these people have gone out from the Church to make it clear
that 'all who are in the Church do not really belong to it'.
As C. H. Dodd puts it, 'Membership of the Church is no
guarantee that a man belongs to Christ and not to Antichrist.'
As A. E. Brooke puts it, although he does not agree that it is
the meaning of the Greek, 'External membership is no proof
of inward union.' As Paul had it, 'For not all Israelites truly
belong to Israel' (Romans 9:6). A time such as had come

upon John's people had its value, for it sifted the false from the true.

In verse 20, John goes on to remind his people that all of them possess knowledge. The people who had gone out were Gnostics, who claimed that there had been given to them a secret, special and advanced knowledge which was not open to the ordinary Christian. John reminds his people that, in matters of faith, the humblest Christian need have no feeling of inferiority to the most learned scholar. There are, of course, matters of technical scholarship, of language and of history which must be the preserve of the experts; but the essentials of the faith are the possession of everyone.

This leads John to his last point in this section. He writes to them, not because they did not know the truth, but because they did. The New Testament scholar B. F. Westcott puts it in this way: 'The object of the apostle in writing was not to communicate fresh knowledge, but to bring into active and decisive use the knowledge which his readers already possessed.' The greatest Christian defence is simply to remember what we know. What we need is not new truth, but for the truth which we already know to become active and effective in our lives.

This is an approach which Paul continually uses. He writes to the Thessalonians: 'Now concerning love of the brothers and sisters, you do not need to have anyone write to you, for you yourselves have been taught by God to love one another' (1 Thessalonians 4:9). What they need is not new truth but to put into practice the truth they already know. He writes to the Romans: 'I myself feel confident about you, my brothers and sisters, that you yourselves are full of goodness, filled with all knowledge, and able to instruct one another. Nevertheless, on some points I have written to you rather boldly by way of reminder, because of the grace given me by God'

(Romans 15:14–15). What they need is not so much to be
taught as to be reminded.

It is the simple fact of the Christian life that things would
be different immediately, if we would only put into practice
what we already know. That is not to say that we never need
to learn anything new; but it is to say that, even as we are, we
have light enough to walk by if we would only use it.

THE SUPREME LIE

1 John 2:22–3

> Who is the liar but the man who denies that Jesus is
> the Anointed One of God? Antichrist is he who denies
> the Father and the Son. Anyone who denies the Son
> does not even have the Father; and everyone who
> acknowledges the Son has the Father also.

To deny that Jesus is the Christ has been described as the
supreme lie – the lie of all lies.

John says that whoever denies the Son does not have the
Father either. What lies behind that saying is this. The false
teachers pleaded: 'It may be that we have different ideas from
yours about *Jesus*; but you and we do believe the same things
about *God*.' John's answer is that that is an impossible
position; no one can deny the Son and still have the Father.
How does he arrive at this view?

He arrives at it because no one who accepts New Testament
teaching can arrive at any other. It is the consistent teaching
of the New Testament, and it is the claim of Jesus himself,
that without him no one can know God. Jesus said quite
clearly that no one knows the Father except the Son and
anyone to whom the Son reveals that knowledge (Matthew
11:27; Luke 10:22). Jesus said: 'Whoever believes in me

believes not in me but in him who sent me. And whoever sees me sees him who sent me' (John 12:44–5). When, towards the end, Philip said that they would be content if Jesus would only show them the Father, Jesus' answer was: 'Whoever has seen me has seen the Father' (John 14:9). It is through Jesus that we know God; it is in Jesus that we can approach God. If we deny Jesus' right to speak, if we deny his special knowledge and his special relationship to God, we can have no more confidence in what he says. His words become no more than the guesses which any good and great person could make. Apart from Jesus, we have no secure knowledge of God; to deny him is at the same time to lose hold of God.

Further, it is Jesus' claim that our reaction to him is, in fact, a reaction to God and that that reaction settles our destiny in time and in eternity. He said: 'Everyone therefore who acknowledges me before others, I also will acknowledge before my Father in heaven; but whoever denies me before others, I also will deny before my Father in heaven' (Matthew 10:32–3). To deny Jesus is to be separated from God, for our relationship to God depends on our reaction to Jesus.

To deny Jesus is indeed the *supreme lie*, for it is to lose entirely the faith and the knowledge which he alone makes possible.

We may say that there are three New Testament confessions of Jesus. There is the confession that he is the *Son of God* (Matthew 16:16; John 9:35–8); there is the confession that he is *Lord* (Philippians 2:11); and there is the confession that he is *Messiah* (1 John 2:22). The essence of every one of them is the affirmation that Jesus stands in a unique relationship to God; and to deny that relationship is to deny the certainty that everything Jesus said about God is true. The Christian faith depends on the unique relationship of

Jesus to God. John is, therefore, right: the person who denies the Son has lost the Father too.

THE UNIVERSAL PRIVILEGE

1 John 2:24–9

> If that which you have heard from the beginning remains within you, you too will remain in the Son and in the Father. And this is the promise which he made to you – eternal life. I am writing these things to you to warn you about those who are seeking to lead you astray. As for you, if that anointing which you have received from him remains in you, you have no need for anyone to teach you. But, as his anointing teaches you about all things and is true and is no lie, and as he has taught you, remain in him. And now, little children, remain in him, so that, if he appears, we may have confidence and not shrink in shame away from him at his coming. If you know that he is righteous, you must be aware that everyone who does righteousness is born of him.

JOHN is pleading with his people to abide in the things which they have learned – for, if they do, they will abide in Christ. The great interest of this passage lies in an expression which John has already used. In verse 20, he has already spoken of the *anointing* which his people had had from the Holy One and through which all of them were equipped with knowledge. Here, he speaks of the anointing which they have received and the anointing which teaches them all things. What is the thought behind this word *anointing*? We shall have to go back some distance in Hebrew thought to discover it.

In Hebrew thought and practice, anointing was connected with three kinds of people. (1) *Priests* were anointed. The ritual regulation runs: 'You shall take the anointing-oil, and pour it on his [the priest's] head and anoint him' (Exodus 29:7; cf. 40:13; Leviticus 16:32). (2) *Kings* were anointed. Samuel anointed Saul as king of the nation (1 Samuel 9:16, 10:1). Later, Samuel anointed David as king (1 Samuel 16:3, 16:12). Elijah was told to anoint Hazael and Jehu (1 Kings 19:15–16). Anointing was the symbol of coronation, as it still is. (3) *Prophets* were anointed. Elijah was told to anoint Elisha as his successor (1 Kings 19:16). The Lord had anointed the prophet Isaiah to bring good tidings to the nation (Isaiah 61:1).

Here, then, is the first significant thing. In the past, anointing had been the privilege of the chosen few, the priests, the prophets and the kings; but now it is the privilege of every Christian, however humble he or she may be. First, the anointing stands for the privilege of all Christians in Jesus Christ.

The high priest was called *the anointed*; but the supreme *Anointed One* was the *Messiah*. (*Messiah* is the Hebrew for *the Anointed One*, and *Christos* is the Greek equivalent.) So, Jesus was supremely *the Anointed One*. The question then arose: when was he anointed? The answer which the Church always gave was that *at his baptism* Jesus was anointed with the Holy Spirit (Acts 10:38).

The Greek world also knew of anointing. Anointing was one of the ceremonies of initiation into the mystery religions, in which people were supposed to gain special knowledge of God. We know that at least some of the false teachers claimed a special anointing which brought them a special knowledge of God. The third-century theologian Hippolytus tells us how these false teachers said: 'We alone of all men are Christians, who complete the mystery at the third portal and are anointed there with speechless anointing.' John's answer is that it is the ordinary Christian who has the only true anointing, the anointing which Jesus gives.

When did that anointing come to Christians, and of what did it consist?

The first question is easy to answer. There was only one ceremony that all Christians passed through, and that was *baptism*; it was, indeed, in later days the standard practice at baptism to anoint Christians with holy oil, as Tertullian, the third-century theologian, tells us.

The second question is not so easy. There are, in fact, two equally possible answers.

(1) It may be that the anointing means the coming of the Spirit upon the Christian in baptism. In the early Church, that happened in the most visible way (Acts 8:17). If in this passage we were to substitute the *Holy Spirit* for *anointing*, it would make excellent sense.

(2) But there is another possibility. Verses 24 and 27 are almost exactly parallel in expression. In verse 24, we read: 'Let what you heard from the beginning abide in you.' And in verse 27, we read: 'The anointing that you received from him abides in you.' The two ideas, *that which you have received from the beginning* and *the anointing*, are exactly parallel. Therefore, it may well be that the anointing which Christians receive is the instruction in the Christian faith, which is given to them when they enter the Church.

It may well be that we do not need to choose between these two interpretations and that they are both present in what John writes. This would mean something very valuable. It would mean that we have two tests by which to judge any new teaching offered to us. (1) Is it in accordance with the Christian tradition which we have been taught? (2) Is it in accordance with the witness of the Holy Spirit speaking within?

Here are the Christian criteria of truth. There is an *external* test. All teaching must be in accordance with the tradition handed down to us in Scripture and in the Church. There is also an *internal* test. All teaching must undergo the test of the Holy Spirit witnessing within our hearts.

ABIDING IN CHRIST

1 John 2:24–9 (*contd*)

BEFORE we leave this passage, we must note two great and practical things in it.

(1) In verse 28, John urges his people to abide continually in Christ so that, when he does come back in power and glory, they may not shrink from him in shame. By far the best way to be ready for the coming of Christ is to live with him every day. If we do that, his coming will not be a shock to us but simply the entry into the nearer presence of one with whom we have lived for a long time.

Even if we have doubts and difficulties about the physical second coming of Christ, this still remains true. For everyone, life will some day come to an end; God's summons comes to all to rise and bid this world farewell. If we have never thought of God, and if Jesus has been only a dim and distant memory, that will be a summons to voyage into a frightening unknown. But, if we have lived consciously in the presence of Christ, if day by day we have talked and walked with God, that will be a summons to come home and to enter into the nearer presence of one who is not a stranger but a friend.

(2) In verse 29, John comes back to a thought which is never far from his mind. The only way in which people can prove that they are abiding in Christ is by the righteousness of their lives. Declarations of faith and loyalty will always be proved or disproved by practice.

REMEMBER THE PRIVILEGES OF THE
CHRISTIAN LIFE

1 John 3:1–2

> See what kind of love the Father has given to us, that
> we should be called the children of God – and such we
> indeed are. The reason why the world does not recognize
> us is that it did not recognize him. Beloved, even as
> things are, we are children of God, and it has not yet
> been made clear what we shall be. We know that, if it
> shall be made clear, we shall be like him because we
> shall see him as he is.

IT may well be that the best illumination of this passage is
the Scottish Paraphrase of it:

> Behold the amazing gift of love
>   the Father hath bestow'd
> On us, the sinful sons of men,
>   to call us sons of God!
>
> Concealed as yet this honour lies,
>   by this dark world unknown,
> A world that knew not when he came,
>   ev'n God's eternal Son.
>
> High is the rank we now possess,
>   but higher we shall rise;
> Though what we shall hereafter be
>   is hid from mortal eyes.
>
> Our souls, we know, when he appears,
>   shall bear his image bright;
> For all his glory, full disclosed,
>   shall open to our sight.

> A hope so great, and so divine,
>   may trials well endure;
> And purge the soul from sense and sin,
>   as Christ himself is pure.

John begins by demanding that his people should remember their privileges. It is their privilege that they are called *the children of God*. There is something even in a name. The fourth-century Church father, John Chrysostom, in a sermon on how to bring up children, advises parents to give their boy some great Scriptural name, to teach him repeatedly the story of the original bearer of the name, and so to give him a standard to live up to when he grows up. So, Christians have the privilege of being called the children of God. Just as to belong to a great school, a great regiment, a great church or a great household is an inspiration in life, so, even more, to bear the name of the family of God is something to keep our feet on the right way and to set us climbing.

But, as John points out, we are not merely *called* the children of God; we *are* the children of God.

There is something here which we may well note. It is by the gift of God that we become children of God. By nature we are God's creatures, but it is by grace that we *become* the children of God. There are two English words which are closely connected but whose meanings are widely different – *paternity* and *fatherhood*. *Paternity* describes a relationship in which a man is responsible for the physical existence of a child; *fatherhood* describes an intimate, loving relationship. In the sense of *paternity*, we are all children of God; but, in the sense of *fatherhood*, we are children of God only when he makes his gracious approach to us and we respond.

There are two pictures, one from the Old Testament and one from the New, which aptly and vividly set out this relationship. In the Old Testament, there is the *covenant idea*.

82

Israel is the covenant people of God. That is to say, God on his own initiative had made a special approach to Israel; he was to be uniquely their God, and they were to be uniquely his people. As an integral part of the covenant, God gave to Israel his law, and it was on the keeping of that law that the covenant relationship depended.

In the New Testament, there is the idea of *adoption* (Romans 8:14-17; 1 Corinthians 1:9; Galatians 3:26-7, 4:6-7). Here is the idea that, by a deliberate act of adoption on the part of God, every Christian enters into his family.

While all men and women are children of God in the sense that they owe their lives to him, they become his children in the intimate and loving sense of the term only by an act of God's initiating grace and the response of their own hearts.

Immediately, the question arises: if people have that great honour when they become Christians, why are they so despised by the world? The answer is that they are experiencing only what Jesus Christ has already experienced. When he came into the world, he was not recognized as the Son of God; the world preferred its own ideas and rejected his. The same is bound to happen to anyone who chooses to embark on the way of Jesus Christ.

REMEMBER THE POSSIBILITIES OF THE CHRISTIAN LIFE

1 John 3:1-2 (*contd*)

So, John begins by reminding his people of the privileges of the Christian life. He goes on to set before them what is in many ways an even more tremendous truth – the great fact that *this life is only a beginning*. Here, John refers to the only true agnosticism. So great is the future and its glory that he will not even guess at it or try to put it into inevitably inadequate words. But there are certain things he does say about it.

(1) When Christ appears in his glory, we shall be like him. Surely, John had in mind the saying of the old creation story that human beings were made in the image and in the likeness of God (Genesis 1:26). That was God's intention, and that was human destiny. We have only to look into any mirror to see how far we have fallen short of that destiny. But John believes that, in Christ, people will finally attain it and at last bear the image and the likeness of God. It is John's belief that only through the work of Christ in their souls can men and women reach the true humanity that God meant them to reach.

(2) When Christ appears, we shall see him and be like him. The goal of all the great Christian men and women has been the vision of God. The end of all devotion is to see God. But that vision of God is not for the sake of intellectual satisfaction; it is in order that we may become like him. There is a paradox here. We cannot become like God unless we see him; and we cannot see him unless we are pure in heart, for only the pure in heart shall see God (Matthew 5:8). In order to see God, we need the purity which only he can give. We are not to think of this vision of God as something which only the great mystics can enjoy. There is somewhere a story about a poor and simple man who would often go into a cathedral to pray; and he would always pray kneeling before the crucifix. Someone noticed that, though he knelt in the attitude of prayer, his lips never moved and he never seemed to say anything, and asked the man what he was doing kneeling like that. The man answered: 'I look at him; and he looks at me.' That is the vision of God in Christ that everyone can have; and whoever looks long enough at Jesus Christ must become like him.

We must note one other thing. John is here thinking in terms of the second coming of Christ. It may be that we can think in the same terms; or it may be that we cannot think so literally of a coming of Christ in glory. Be that as it may, there will come for every one of us the day when we shall see Christ and behold his glory. Here, there is always the veil of sense and time; but the day will come when that veil, too, will be torn in two. As Ray Palmer's hymn has it,

> When death these mortal eyes shall seal,
> And still this throbbing heart,
> The rending veil shall thee reveal
> All glorious as thou art.

Therein is the Christian hope and the vast possibility that the Christian life holds for us.

THE OBLIGATION OF PURITY

1 John 3:3–8

Anyone who rests this hope on him purifies himself as he is pure. Anyone who commits sin commits lawlessness, and sin is lawlessness. And you know that he appeared that he might take away our sins and there is no sin in him. Anyone who abides in him does not sin. Anyone who sins has not seen him, and does not know him. Little children, let no one deceive you. He who does righteousness is righteous, even as he is righteous. He who does sin is of the devil, because the devil is a sinner from the beginning. The purpose for which the Son of God appeared was that he might destroy the works of the devil.

JOHN has just said that Christians are on the way to seeing God and being like him. There is nothing like a great aim for helping people to resist temptation. A novelist draws the picture of a young man who always refused to share in the lower pleasures to which his friends often invited and even urged him. His explanation was that, some day, something fine was going to come to him, and he must keep himself ready for it. Those who know that God stands at the end of the road will make all life a preparation to meet him.

This passage is directed against the Gnostic false teachers. As we have seen, they produced more than one reason to justify sin. They said that the body was evil and that, therefore, there was no harm in satisfying its lusts to the full, because what happened to it was of no importance. They said that truly spiritual people were protected to such an extent by the Spirit that they could sin to their hearts' content and come to no harm. They even said that there was an obligation on true Gnostics both to scale the heights and to plumb the depths so that they might be truly said to know all things. Behind John's answer, there is a kind of analysis of sin.

He begins by insisting that no one is above the moral law. No one can say that it is quite safe to indulge in certain things, although they may be dangerous for others. In his commentary, A. E. Brooke puts it like this: 'The test of progress is obedience.' Progress does not confer the privilege to sin; the further on we are, the more disciplined we must be. John goes on to imply certain basic truths about sin.

(1) He tells us *what sin is*. It is the deliberate breaking of a law of which people are well aware. Sin is to obey oneself rather than to obey God.

(2) He tells us *what sin does*. It undoes the work of Christ. Christ is the Lamb of God who takes away the sins of the world (John 1:29). To sin is to bring back what he came into the world to abolish.

86

(3) He tells us *why sin is*. It comes from the failure to abide in Christ. We need not think that this is a truth only for advanced mystics. It simply means this: as long as we remember the continual presence of Jesus, we will not sin; it is when we forget that presence that we sin.

(4) He tells us *where sin comes from*. It comes from the devil; and the devil is the one who sins, as it were, on principle. That is probably the meaning of the phrase *from the beginning* (verse 8). We sin for the pleasure that we think it will bring to us; the devil sins as a matter of principle. The New Testament does not try to explain the devil and his origin; but it is quite convinced – and it is a fact of universal experience – that in the world there is a power hostile to God, and to sin is to obey that power instead of God.

(5) He tells us how *sin is conquered*. It is conquered because Jesus Christ destroyed the works of the devil. The New Testament often dwells on the Christ who faced and conquered the powers of evil (Matthew 12:25–9; Luke 10:18; Colossians 2:15; 1 Peter 3:22; John 12:31). He has broken the power of evil, and by his help that same victory can be ours.

THOSE WHO HAVE BEEN BORN OF GOD

1 John 3:9

> Anyone who has been born of God does not commit sin, because his seed abides in him; and he cannot be a consistent and deliberate sinner, because he has been born of God.

THIS verse bristles with difficulties, and yet it is obviously of great importance to find out what it means.

First, what does John mean by the phrase '*because his seed abides in him*'? There are three possibilities.

(1) The Bible frequently uses the word *seed* to mean a man's family and descendants. The Authorized Version tells us that Abraham and his *seed* are to keep the covenant of God (Genesis 17:9). God made his promise to Abraham and to his *seed* forever (Luke 1:55). The Jews claim to be Abraham's *seed* (John 8:33, 8:37). In Galatians 3, Paul speaks about Abraham's *seed* (Galatians 3:16, 3:29). If we take *seed* in that sense here, we need to take *him* as referring to God, and then we get very good sense. 'Anyone who has been born of God does not sin, because God's family constantly abide in God.' God's family live so near to God that they may be said to abide in him. All who live like that have a strong defence against sin.

(2) It is human seed which produces human life, and children may be said to have their father's seed in them. Now, Christians are reborn through God and, therefore, have God's seed in them. This was an idea with which the people of John's time were very familiar. The Gnostics said that God had sowed seeds into this world, and, through the action of these seeds, the world was being perfected; and they claimed that it was the true Gnostics who had received these seeds. Some Gnostics said that the human body was a material and evil thing; but into some bodies Wisdom secretly sowed seeds, and the truly spiritual people have these seeds of God for souls. This was closely connected with the Stoic belief that God was fiery spirit and that the soul, which gave life and reason to the individual, was a spark (*scintilla*) of that divine fire which had come from God to reside in the body.

If we take John's words this way, it means that all who are reborn have the seed of God in them, and that therefore they cannot sin. There is no doubt that John's readers would be familiar with this idea.

(3) There is a much simpler idea. Twice at least in the New Testament, *the word of God* is that which is said to bring rebirth to men and women. James has it: 'In fulfilment of his own purpose he gave us birth by the word of truth, so that we would become a kind of first fruits of his creatures' (James 1:18). The word of God is like the seed of God which produces new life. Peter has this idea even more clearly: 'You have been born anew, not of perishable but of imperishable seed, through the living and enduring word of God' (1 Peter 1:23). There, *the word of God* is definitely identified with *the imperishable seed of God*. If we take it this way, John means that those who are born of God cannot sin because they have the strength and guidance of the word of God within them. This third way is simplest and, on the whole, best. Christians are preserved from sin by the indwelling power of the word of God.

THOSE WHO CANNOT SIN

1 John 3:9 (*contd*)

SECOND, this verse presents us with the problem of relating it to certain other things which John has already said about sin. Let us set the verse down, as it is in the New Revised Standard Version:

> Those who have been born of God do not sin, because
> God's seed abides in them; they cannot sin, because
> they have been born of God.

Taken at its face value, this means that it is impossible for anyone who is born of God to sin. Now, John has already said: 'If we say that we have no sin, we deceive ourselves, and the truth is not in us' and: 'If we say that we have not sinned, we make him [i.e. God] a liar'; and he urges us to confess our sins (I John 1:8, 1:10). He goes on to say: 'If anyone does sin, we have an advocate with the Father, [in the person of] Jesus Christ' (2:1). On the face of it, there is contradiction here. In the one place, John is saying that we cannot be anything other than sinners and that there is an atonement for our sin. In the other place, he is saying equally definitely that those who are born of God cannot sin. What is the explanation?

(1) John inevitably thinks in Jewish categories. We have already seen that he knew and accepted the Jewish picture of the two ages, *this present age* and *the age to come*. We have also seen that it was John's belief that, whatever the world was like, Christians by virtue of the work of Christ had already entered into the new age. It was exactly one of the characteristics of the new age that those who lived in it would be free from sin. In I Enoch, we read: 'Then too will wisdom be bestowed on the elect, and they will all live and *never again sin*, either through heedlessness or through pride' (I Enoch 5:8). If that is true of the new age, it ought to be true of Christians who are living in it. But, in fact, it is still not true because Christians have not yet escaped from the power of sin. We might then say that, in this passage, John is setting down the *ideal* of what should be, and in the other two passages he is facing the *actuality* of what is. We might say that he knows the ideal and confronts men and women with it; but he also faces the facts and sees the cure in Christ for them.

(2) That may well be so; but there is more to it. In the Greek, there is a subtle difference in tenses which gives a very wide difference in meaning. In I John 2:1, it is John's command *that you may not sin*. In that verse, *sin* is in the

aorist tense, which indicates a particular and definite act. So, what John is saying is quite clearly that Christians must not commit individual acts of sin; but, if they do lapse into sin, they have in Christ an advocate to plead their cause and a sacrifice to atone for that sin. On the other hand, in our present passage, in both cases, *sin* is in the *present* tense and indicates habitual action.

What John is saying may be put down in four stages. (a) The ideal is that, in the new age, sin is gone forever. (b) Christians must try to make that true and, with the help of Christ, struggle to avoid individual acts of sin. (c) In fact, we all have these lapses – and, when we do, we must humbly confess them to God, who will always forgive the penitent heart. (d) In spite of that, Christians cannot possibly be deliberate and consistent sinners; Christians cannot live a life in which sin dominates their actions.

John is not setting before us a terrifying perfectionism; but he is demanding a life which is always on the watch against sin, a life in which sin is not the normal accepted way but the abnormal moment of defeat. John is not saying that those who abide in God cannot sin; but he is saying that those who abide in God cannot continue to be deliberate sinners.

THE MARKS OF THE CHILDREN OF GOD

1 John 3:10–18

> In this, the children of God and the children of the devil are made plain; anyone who does not do righteousness is not of God, and neither is he who does not love his brother, because the message that we have heard from the beginning is the message that we should love one another, that we should not be like Cain, who was of

the evil one and slew his brother. And why did he slay
him? Because his works were evil and his brother's
works were just. Do not be surprised, brothers, if the
world hates you. We know that we have passed from
death to life, because we love the brothers. He who does
not love remains in death. Anyone who hates his brother
is a murderer. He does not possess eternal life abiding
within him. In this we recognize his love, that he laid
down his life for us; and we ought to lay down our life
for the brothers. Whoever possesses enough for his
livelihood in this world and sees his brother in need
and shuts his heart against him, how does the love of
God abide in him? My dear children, do not make love
a matter of talking and of the tongue, but love in deed
and in truth.

THIS is a passage with a close-knit argument with an additional
point – a kind of insertion in the middle.

As the scholar B. F. Westcott has it, 'Life reveals the
children of God.' We can tell what a tree is by its fruits, and
similarly we can tell what a man or woman is by that person's
conduct. John lays it down that anyone who does not do what
is right is by that fact shown not to be of God. At present, we
shall leave out the inserted point and go straight on with the
argument.

Although John is a mystic, he has a very practical mind;
and, therefore, he will not leave righteousness vague and
undefined. Someone might say: 'Very well, I accept the fact
that the only thing which proves that people belong to God is
the righteousness of their lives. But what is righteousness?'
John's answer is clear and unequivocal. *To be righteous is to
love our neighbours.* That, says John, is a duty about which
we should never be in any doubt. And he goes on to produce
various reasons why that commandment is so central and so
binding.

(1) It is a duty which has been impressed upon Christians from the first moment that they entered the Church. The Christian ethic can be summed up in the one word *love* – and, from the moment that people commit themselves to Christ, they commit themselves to lives in which the driving force is love.

(2) For that very reason, the fact that people love one another is the final proof that they have passed from death to life. As A. E. Brooke comments on this passage, 'Life is a chance of learning how to love.' Life without love is death. To love is to be in the light; to hate is to remain in the dark. We need no further proof of that than to look at the face of someone who is in love and the face of someone who is full of hate; it will show the glory or the deep darkness in that person's heart.

(3) Further, not to love is to become a murderer. There can be no doubt that John is thinking of the words of Jesus in the Sermon on the Mount (Matthew 5:21–2). Jesus said that the old law forbade murder; but the new law declared that anger and bitterness and contempt were sins that were just as serious. Whenever there is hatred in the heart, an individual becomes a potential murderer. To allow hatred to settle in the heart is to break a definite commandment of Jesus. Therefore, the one who loves is a follower of Christ, and the one who hates is no follower of his.

(4) There follows still another step in this close-knit argument. Someone may say: 'I admit this obligation of love and I will try to fulfil it; but I do not know what it involves.' John's answer (verse 16) is: 'If you want to see what this love is, look at Jesus Christ. In his death for us on the cross, it is fully displayed.' In other words, the Christian life is the imitation of Christ. 'Let the same mind be in you that was in Christ Jesus' (Philippians 2:5). 'Christ also suffered for you,

leaving you an example, so that you should follow in his steps' (1 Peter 2:21). No one can look at Christ and then claim not to know what the Christian life is.

(5) John meets one more possible objection. Someone may say: 'How can I follow in the steps of Christ? He laid down his life upon the cross. You say I ought to lay down my life for others. But opportunities as dramatic as that do not come into my life. What then?' John's answer is: 'True. But when you see someone who is in need and you have enough, to give that person from what you have is to follow Christ. To shut your heart and to refuse to give is to show that the love of God which was in Jesus Christ has no place in you.'

John insists that we can find plenty of opportunities to reveal the love of Christ in everyday life. C. H. Dodd writes impressively on this passage: 'There were occasions in the life of the early church, as there are certainly tragic occasions at the present day, for a quite literal obedience to this precept, [that is, to lay down our life for the brothers]. But not all life is tragic; and yet the same principle of conduct must apply all through. Thus it may call for the simple expenditure of money we might have spent upon ourselves, to relieve the need of someone poorer. It is, after all, the same principle of action, though at a lower level of intensity: it is the willingness to surrender that which has value for our own life, to enrich the life of another. If such a minimum response to the law of charity, called for by such an everyday situation, is absent, then it is idle to pretend we are within the family of God, the realm in which love is operative as the principle and the token of eternal life.'

Fine words will never take the place of fine deeds; and no amount of talk of Christian love will take the place of a kindly action to someone in need, made at some personal expense or with some self-sacrifice, for in that action the principle of the cross is at work again.

THE WORLD'S RESENTMENT OF THE CHRISTIAN WAY

1 John 3:10–18 (*contd*)

In this passage, there is an insertion; we return to it now. The additional point is made in verse 11, and the conclusion drawn from it is in verse 12. Christians must not be like Cain, who murdered his brother. John goes on to ask why Cain murdered his brother; and his answer is that it was because his works were evil and his brother's were good. Then he drops the remark: 'Do not be surprised, brothers, if the world hates you.'

An evil person will instinctively hate a good person. Righteousness always provokes hostility in the minds of those whose actions are evil. The reason is that the good person is a walking rebuke to the evil person. Even if they never speak a word to one another, the good person's life passes a silent judgment. Socrates was the supreme example of the good man; Alcibiades was brilliant but erratic and often debauched. He used to say to Socrates: 'Socrates, I hate you, because every time I meet you, you show me what I am.'

The Wisdom of Solomon has a grim passage (2:12–16). In it, those who are evil are made to express their attitude to the good man: 'Let us lie in wait for the righteous man; because he is inconvenient to us and opposes our actions . . . He became to us a reproof of our thoughts; the very sight of him is a burden to us, because his manner of life is unlike that of others, and his ways are strange. We are considered by him as something base, and he avoids our ways as unclean.' The very sight of the good man made evil people hate him.

Wherever Christians are, even though they say nothing, they act as the conscience of society; and, for that very reason, the world will often hate them.

In ancient Athens, the noble Aristides was unjustly banished; and, when one member of the jury was asked how he could have cast his vote against such a man, his answer was that he was tired of hearing Aristides called 'the Just'. The hatred of the world for Christians is a phenomenon that is always with us, and it is due to the fact that in Christians people with worldly values see themselves condemned; they see in Christians what they are not and what deep down they know they ought to be; and, because they will not change, they seek to eliminate those who remind them of the lost goodness.

THE ONLY TEST

I John 3:19–24a

> By this we know that we are of the truth, and by this we will reassure our heart before him, when our heart condemns us in anything, for God is greater than our hearts and knows all things. Beloved, if our heart does not condemn us, we can come confidently to God and receive from him whatever we ask, because we keep his commandments and do the things which are well pleasing to him. And this is his commandment, that we should believe in the name of his Son Jesus Christ and that we should love one another, even as he gave us his commandment. And he who keeps his commandment abides in him and he in him.

INTO every human heart, there are bound to come doubts. It is natural for people with any sensitivity of mind or heart to wonder at times if they really are Christians. John's test is quite simple and far-reaching. It is love. If we feel love for our neighbours welling up within our hearts, we can be sure that the heart of Christ is in us. John would have said that a so-called heretic whose heart was overflowing with love and whose life had an attractive quality in the service of others was far nearer Christ than someone who was impeccably orthodox, yet cold and remote from the needs of others.

John goes on to say something which, as far as the Greek goes, can mean two things. That feeling of love can reassure us in the presence of God. Our hearts may condemn us; but God is greater than our hearts. The question is: what is the meaning of this last phrase?

(1) It could mean: since our hearts condemn us and God is infinitely greater than our hearts, God must condemn us even more. If we take it that way, it leaves us only with the fear of God and with nothing to say but: 'God be merciful to me, a sinner.' That is a possible translation, and no doubt it is true; but it is not what John is saying in this context, for here he is thinking of our confidence in God and not our dread of him.

(2) The passage must therefore mean this. Our hearts condemn us – that is inevitable. But God is greater than our hearts; he knows all things. Not only does he know our sins; he also knows our love, our longings, the nobility that never fully works itself out, our penitence; and the greatness of his knowledge gives him the sympathy which can understand and forgive.

It is this very knowledge of God which gives us our hope. 'Man', as the thirteenth-century scholar Thomas Aquinas said, 'sees the deed, but God knows the intention.' Other people can judge us only by our actions, but God can judge us by the longings which never became deeds and the dreams which never came true.

When Solomon was dedicating the Temple, he spoke of how David had wanted to build a house for God and how that privilege had been denied to him. 'My father David had it in mind to build a house for the name of the Lord, the God of Israel. But the Lord said to my father, "You did well to consider building a house for my name"' (1 Kings 8:17–18).

The French proverb says: 'To know all is to forgive all.' God judges us by the deep emotions of the heart; and, if in our heart there is love, then, however feeble and imperfect that love may be, we can with confidence enter into his presence. The perfect knowledge which belongs to God, and to God alone, is not our terror but our hope.

THE INSEPARABLE COMMANDS

1 John 3:19–24a (*contd*)

JOHN goes on to speak of the two things which are well-pleasing in God's sight, the two commandments on obedience on which our relationship to God depends.

(1) We must believe in the name of his Son Jesus Christ. Here, we have that use of the word *name* which is peculiar to the biblical writers. It does not mean simply the name by which a person is called; it means the whole nature and character of that person as far as it is known to us. The psalmist writes: 'Our help is in the name of the Lord' (Psalm 124:8). Clearly, that does not mean that our help lies in the fact that God is called Yahweh; it means that our help is in the love and mercy and power which have been revealed to us as the nature and character of God. So, to believe in the

name of Jesus Christ means to believe in the nature and character of Jesus Christ. It means to believe that he is the Son of God, that he does stand in relation to God in a way in which no other person in the universe ever stood or ever can stand, that he can perfectly reveal God to us and that he is the Saviour of our souls. To believe in the name of Jesus Christ is to accept him for what he really is.

(2) We must love one another, even as he gave us his commandment. This commandment is in John 13:34. We must love each other with that same selfless, sacrificial, forgiving love with which Jesus Christ loved us.

When we put these two commandments together, we find the great truth that the Christian life depends on the combination of right belief and right conduct. We cannot have the one without the other. There can be no such thing as a Christian theology without a Christian ethic; and equally there can be no such thing as a Christian ethic without a Christian theology. Our belief is not real belief unless it is translated into action; and our action has neither authority nor force unless it is based on belief.

We cannot begin the Christian life until we accept Jesus Christ for what he is; and we have not accepted him in any real sense of the term until our attitude to others is the same as his own attitude of love.

THE PERILS OF THE SURGING LIFE OF THE SPIRIT

1 John 3:24b–4:1

This is how we know that he abides in us, by the Spirit which he gave to us. Beloved, do not believe every spirit, but test the spirits to see if their source is God,

because many false prophets have gone out into the
world.

BEHIND this warning is a situation of which we in the modern
Church know little or nothing. In the early Church, there
was a surging life of the Spirit which brought its own perils.
There were so many and such diverse spiritual manifestations
that some kind of test was necessary. Let us try to think
ourselves back into that electric atmosphere.

(1) Even in Old Testament times, people realized the
dangers presented by false prophets who possessed spiritual
power. Deuteronomy 13:1–5 demands that false prophets
who sought to lure people away from the true God should
be put to death; but it frankly and freely admits that such
prophets may promise signs and wonders and perform them.
The spiritual power is there, but it is evil and misdirected.

(2) In the early Church, the spiritual world was very near.
All the world believed in a universe thronged with demons
and spirits. Every rock and tree and river, every wood, lake
and mountain had its spiritual power; and these spiritual powers
were always seeking entry into the bodies and minds of men
and women. In the time of the early Church, people lived in a
haunted world, and there had never been a time when they
were so conscious of being surrounded by spiritual powers.

(3) That ancient world was very conscious of a personal
power of evil. It did not speculate about its source, but it was
sure that it was there and that it was seeking for individuals
who might be its instruments. It follows that not only the
universe but also the minds of men and women provided the
battle ground on which the power of the light and the power
of the dark fought out the issue.

(4) In the early Church, the coming of the Spirit was a much
more visible phenomenon than is common nowadays. It was

usually connected with baptism; and, when the Spirit came, things happened that anyone could see. The person who received the Spirit was visibly affected. When the apostles came down to Samaria, after the preaching of Philip, and brought the gift of the Spirit to the new converts, the effects were so startling that the local magician, Simon Magus, wished to buy the power to produce the same effect (Acts 8:17–18). The coming of the Spirit on Cornelius and his people was something that anyone could see (Acts 10:44–5). In the early Church, there was an ecstatic element in the coming of the Spirit, whose effects were violent and obvious.

(5) This had its effect in the congregational life of the early Church. The best commentary on this passage of John is, in fact, 1 Corinthians 14. Because of the power of the Spirit, people spoke with tongues. That is to say, they poured out a flood of Spirit-given sounds in no known language, which no one could understand unless there was someone present who had the Spirit-given power to interpret. So extraordinary was this phenomenon that Paul does not hesitate to say that, if strangers came into a congregation in which it was in action, they would think that they had arrived in a community that had gone mad (1 Corinthians 14:2, 23, 27). Even the prophets, who delivered their message in plain language, were a problem. They were so moved by the Spirit that they could not wait for each other to finish, and they would leap to their feet determined to shout out their own Spirit-given message (1 Corinthians 14:26–7, 33). A service of worship in an early Christian congregation was very different from the calm of most modern church services. So diverse were the manifestations of the Spirit that Paul numbers the *discerning of spirits* among the spiritual gifts which a Christian might possess (1 Corinthians 12:10). We can see what might happen in such a case when Paul speaks

of the possibility of someone saying in a spirit that Christ is accursed (I Corinthians 12:3).

When we come further down in Christian history, we find the problem still more acute. The *Didache*, or *The Teaching of the Twelve Apostles*, is the first service order book and is usually dated just after AD 100. It has regulations on how to deal with the wandering apostles and prophets who came and went among the Christian congregations. 'Not everyone who speaks in a spirit is a prophet; he is only a prophet if he walks in the ways of the Lord' (*Didache*, 11–12). The matter reached its absolute peak when, in the third century, Montanus burst upon the Church with the claim that he was nothing less than the promised Paraclete and that he proposed to tell the Church the things which Christ had said his apostles could not at the moment bear.

The early Church was full of this surging life of the Spirit. The exuberance of life had not been organized out of the Church. It was a great age; but its very exuberance had its dangers. If there was a personal power of evil, men and women could be used by that power. If there were evil spirits as well as the Holy Spirit, individuals could be occupied by them. People could delude themselves into a quite subjective experience in which they thought – quite honestly – that they had a message from the Spirit.

All this is in John's mind; and it is in the context of that surging atmosphere of pulsating spiritual life that he sets out his criteria to judge between the true and the false. We, for our part, may well feel that with all its dangers, the exuberant vitality of the early Church was a far better thing than the apathetic calmness of so much of the life of the modern Church. It was surely better to expect the Spirit everywhere than nowhere.

Note on the Translation of 1 John 4:1–7

There is a recurring Greek phrase in this passage which is by no means easy to translate. It is the phrase which the Revised Standard Version consistently renders *of God*. Its occurrences are as follows:

Verse 1: Test the spirits to see whether they are *of God*.

Verse 2: Every spirit which confesses that Jesus Christ has come in the flesh is *of God*.

Verse 3: Every spirit which does not confess Jesus Christ is not *of God*.

Verse 4: Little children, you are *of God*.

Verse 6: We are *of God* . . . He who is not *of God* does not listen to us.

Verse 7: Love is *of God*.

The difficulty can be seen in the solutions to which various translators are driven.

James Moffatt, in verses 1–3, translates the phrase as *comes from God*, and in verses 4, 6 and 7 *belongs to God*.

In *The New Testament in Modern Speech*, R. F. Weymouth, in verses 1–3, translates as *is from God*. In verse 4, he translates: *You are God's children*. In verse 6, he translates: 'We are *God's children* . . . He who is not *a child of God* does not listen to us.' In verse 7, he has: 'Love *has its origin in God*.'

In his *The New Testament in Plain English*, in every case except verse 7, Charles Kingsley Williams translates as *from God*; in verse 7, he has *of God*.

The difficulty is easy to see; and yet it is of prime importance to be able to attach a precise meaning to this phrase. The Greek is *ek tou theou*. *Ho theos* means *God*, and *tou theou* is the genitive case after the preposition *ek*. *Ek* is one of the most common Greek prepositions and means *out of* or *from*. To say that someone came *ek tēs poleōs* would mean that that person came either *out of* or *from* the city. What then does it mean that a person, or a spirit, or a quality is *ek tou theou*? The simplest translation is *from God*. But what does *from* mean in that phrase? Quite certainly, it means that the person, the spirit or the quality *has its origin in God*. It comes from God in the sense that it takes its origin in him and its life from him. So John, for instance, tells his people to test the spirits to see whether they really have their source in God. Love, he says, has its origin in God.

THE ULTIMATE HERESY

1 John 4:2–3

> This is how you recognize the spirit whose source is God. Every spirit which openly acknowledges that Jesus has come in the flesh and is Christ has its origin in God. And every spirit which is such that it does not make this confession about Jesus has not its source in God; and this is the spirit of antichrist, about which you heard that it was to come and which is now here present in the world.

For John, Christian belief could be summed up in one great sentence: 'The Word became flesh and lived among us' (John 1:14). Any spirit which denied the reality of the incarnation was not of God. John lays down two tests of belief.

(1) To be of God, a spirit must acknowledge that Jesus is the Christ, the Messiah. As John saw it, to deny that is to deny three things about Jesus. (a) It is to deny that he is the centre of history, the one for whom all previous history had

been a preparation. (b) It is to deny that he is the fulfilment of the promises of God. All through their struggles and their defeats, the Jews had clung to the promises of God. To deny that Jesus is the promised Messiah is to deny that these promises were true. (c) It is to deny his kingship. Jesus came, not only to sacrifice, but to reign; and to deny his Messiahship is to leave out his essential kingliness.

(2) To be of God, a spirit must acknowledge that Jesus has come in the flesh. It was precisely this that the Gnostics could never accept. Since, in their view, matter was altogether evil, a real incarnation was an impossibility, for God could never take flesh upon himself. St Augustine was later to say that in the Platonist philosophers he could find parallels for everything in the New Testament except for one saying: 'The Word became flesh.' As John saw it, to deny the complete humanity of Jesus Christ was to strike at the very roots of the Christian faith.

To deny the reality of the incarnation has certain definite consequences.

(1) It is to deny that Jesus can ever be our example. If he was not in any real sense a man, living under the same conditions as other men and women, he cannot show them how to live.

(2) It is to deny that Jesus can be the high priest who opens the way to God. The true high priest, as the writer to the Hebrews saw, must be like us in all things, knowing our weaknesses and our temptations (Hebrews 4:14–15). To lead people to God, the high priest must be human, or else he will be pointing them to a road which it is impossible for them to take.

(3) It is to deny that Jesus can in any real sense be Saviour. To save men and women, he had to identify himself with those he came to save.

(4) It is to deny the salvation of the body. Christian teaching is quite clear that salvation is the salvation of the whole person. The body as well as the soul is saved. To deny the incarnation is to deny the possibility that the body can ever become the temple of the Holy Spirit.

(5) By far the most serious and terrible thing is that to deny the incarnation is to deny that there can ever be any real union between God and human beings. If spirit is altogether good and the body is altogether evil, God and humanity can never meet, as long as we are human. They might meet when we have cast off the body and become *disembodied* spirits. But the great truth of the incarnation is that here and now there can be real communion between God and humanity.

Nothing in Christianity is more central than the reality of the humanity of Jesus Christ.

THE SPLIT BETWEEN THE WORLD AND GOD

1 John 4:4–6

> You have your origin in God, dear children, and you have won the victory over them, because that power which is in you is greater than the power which is in the world. This is why the source of their speaking is the world, and is the reason why the world listens to them. Our source is God. He who knows God listens to us. He who has not his source in God does not listen to us. This is how we know the spirit of truth and the spirit of error.

JOHN lays down a great truth and faces a great problem.

(1) Christians need not fear the heretics. In Christ, the victory over all the powers of evil was won. The powers of

evil did their worst to him, even to the extreme of killing him on a cross, and in the end he emerged victorious. That victory belongs to Christians. Whatever things may look like, the powers of evil are fighting a losing battle. As the Latin proverb has it, 'Great is the truth, and in the end it will prevail.' All that Christians have to do is remember the truth they already know and cling to it. The truth is that by which we live; error is ultimately that by which we die.

(2) The problem remains that the false teachers will neither listen to nor accept the truth which true Christians offer. How is that to be explained? John returns to his favourite contrasting theme, the opposition between the world and God. The world, as we have seen before, is human nature apart from, and in opposition to, God. Those who have their source in God will welcome the truth; those whose source is the world will reject the truth.

When we come to think of it, that is obvious. How can anyone who believes that the basis of life is competition even begin to understand an ethic whose keynote is service? How can someone whose aim is the advancement of the self, and who holds that the weakest must go to the wall, even begin to understand a teaching whose principle for living is love? How can someone who believes that this is the only world and that, therefore, material things are the only ones which matter even begin to understand life lived in the light of eternity, where the unseen things have the greatest values? Many people hear only what they want or allow themselves to hear, and they can easily make it impossible for themselves to hear the Christian message.

That is what John is saying. We have seen again and again that it is characteristic of him to see things in terms of black and white. His thinking does not deal in shades. On the one side, there is the person whose source and origin is God and who can hear the truth; on the other side, there is the person whose source and origin is the world and who is incapable of hearing the truth. There emerges a problem, which John probably did not even consider. Are there people to whom all preaching is quite useless? Are there people whose defences can never be broken down, whose deafness can never be penetrated, and whose minds are forever shut to the invitation and command of Jesus Christ?

The answer must be that there are no limits to the grace of God and that there is such a person as the Holy Spirit. It is the lesson of life that the love of God can break every barrier down. It is true that we can resist; it is, maybe, true that we can resist even to the end. But what is also true is that Christ is always knocking at the door of every heart, and it is possible for anyone to hear the voice of Christ, even above the many voices of the world.

LOVE HUMAN AND DIVINE

1 John 4:7–21

> Beloved, let us love one another, because love has its source in God, and everyone who loves has God as the source of his birth and knows God. He who does not love has not come to know God. In this, God's love is displayed within us, that God sent his only Son into the world that through him we might live. In this is love, not that we love God, but that he loved us and sent his Son to be an atoning sacrifice for our sins. Brothers, if God so loved us, we too ought to love each other. No one has ever seen God. If we love each other, God dwells in us and his love is perfected in us. It is by this that we know that we dwell in him and he in us, because he has given us a share of his Spirit. We have seen and

we testify that the Father sent the Son as the Saviour of the world. Whoever openly acknowledges that Jesus is the Son of God, God dwells in him and he in God. We have come to know and to put our trust in the love which God has within us. God is love, and he who dwells in love dwells in God and God dwells in him. With us, love finds its peak in this, that we should have confidence in the day of judgment because, even as he is, so also are we in this world. There is no fear in love; but perfect love casts out fear, for fear is connected with punishment, and he who fears has not reached love's perfect state. We love because he first loved us. If anyone says 'I love God' and hates his brother, he is a liar; for he who does not love his brother, whom he has seen, cannot love God whom he has not seen. It is this command that we have from him, that he who loves God loves his brother also.

THIS passage is so closely interwoven that it is best to read as a whole and then bit by bit to draw out its teaching. First of all, let us look at its teaching on love.

(1) Love has its origin in God (verse 7). It is from the God who is love that all love takes its source. As A. E. Brooke puts it, 'Human love is a reflection of something in the divine nature itself.' We are never nearer to God than when we love. Clement of Alexandria said, in a startling phrase, that the real Christian 'practises being God'. Those who dwell in love dwell in God (verse 16). We are made in the image and the likeness of God (Genesis 1:26). God is love; and, therefore, to be like God and be what we were meant to be, we must also love.

(2) Love has a double relationship to God. It is only by knowing God that we learn to love, and it is only by loving that we learn to know God (verses 7–8). Love comes from God, and love leads to God.

(3) It is by love that God is known (verse 12). We cannot see God, because he is spirit; what we can see is his effect. We cannot see the wind, but we can see what it can do. We cannot see electricity, but we can see the effect it produces. The effect of God is love. It is when God comes into an individual that that person is clothed with the love of God and the love of other people. God is known by his effect on that individual. It has been said that 'a saint is someone in whom Christ lives again'; and the best demonstration of God comes not from argument but from a life of love.

(4) God's love is demonstrated in Jesus Christ (verse 9). When we look at Jesus, we see two things about the love of God. (a) It is a love which holds nothing back. In his love for men and women, God was prepared to give his only Son and make a sacrifice beyond which no sacrifice can possibly go. (b) It is a totally undeserved love. It would be no wonder if we loved God, when we remember all the gifts he has given to us, even apart from Jesus Christ; the wonder is that he loves poor and disobedient creatures like us. As F. W. Faber's hymn has it,

> How thou canst think so well of us,
>   And be the God thou art,
> Is darkness to my intellect,
>   But sunshine to my heart.

(5) Human love is a response to divine love (verse 19). We love because God loved us. It is the sight of his love which wakens in us the desire to love him as he first loved us and to love our neighbours as he loves them.

(6) When love comes, fear goes (verses 17–18). Fear is the characteristic emotion of someone who expects to be punished. As long as we regard God as the Judge, the King

and the Law-giver, there can be nothing in our hearts but fear, for from such a God we can expect nothing but punishment. But once we know God's true nature, fear is swallowed up in love. The fear that remains is the fear of causing him grief in his love for us.

(7) Love of God and love of other people are indissolubly connected (verses 7, 11, 20–1). As C. H. Dodd admirably puts it, 'The energy of love discharges itself along lines which form a triangle, whose points are God, self, and neighbour.' If God loves us, we are bound to love each other, because it is our destiny to reproduce the life of God in humanity and the life of eternity in time. John says, with almost crude bluntness, that anyone who claims to love God and hates a brother or sister is nothing but a liar. The only way to prove that we love God is to love the men and women whom God loves. The only way to prove that God is within our hearts is constantly to show the love for others within our lives.

GOD IS LOVE

1 John 4:7–21 (*contd*)

IN this passage, there occurs what is probably the greatest single statement about God in the whole Bible, that *God is love*. It is amazing how many doors that single statement unlocks and how many questions it answers.

(1) It is the explanation of *creation*. Sometimes we are bound to wonder why God created this world. The disobedience and the lack of response in human beings is a continual grief to him. Why should he create a world which was to bring him nothing but trouble? The answer is that creation was essential to his very nature. If God is love, he

cannot exist in lonely isolation. Love must have someone to love and someone to love it.

(2) It is the explanation of *free will*. Unless love is a free response, it is not love. Had God been only law, he could have created a world in which people moved like robots, having no more choice than a machine. But, if God had made people like that, there would have been no possibility of a personal relationship between him and them. Love is of necessity the free response of the heart; and, therefore, God, by a deliberate act of self-limitation, had to endow men and women with free will.

(3) It is the explanation of *providence*. Had God been simply mind and order and law, he might, so to speak, have created the universe, wound it up, set it going and left it. There are gadgets and pieces of equipment which we are urged to buy because we can install them and forget them; their most attractive quality is that they can be left to run themselves. But, because God is love, his creating act is followed by his constant care.

(4) It is the explanation of *redemption*. If God had been only law and justice, he would simply have left men and women to the consequences of their sin. The moral law would operate; the soul that sinned would die; and the eternal justice would inexorably hand out its punishments. But the very fact that God is love meant that he had to seek out and to save the lost. He had to find a remedy for sin.

(5) It is the explanation of the *life beyond*. If God were simply creator, human beings might live their brief span and die forever. The life which ended early would be only another flower which the frost of death had withered too soon. But the fact that God is love makes it certain that the chances and changes of life do not have the last word and that his love will readjust the balance of this life.

SON OF GOD AND SAVIOUR

1 John 4:7–21 (*contd*)

BEFORE we leave this passage, we must note that it also has great things to say about Jesus Christ.

(1) It tells us that Jesus is *the bringer of life*. God sent him that through him we might have life (verse 9). There is a world of difference between existence and life. We all have existence, but we do not all have life. The very eagerness with which people seek pleasure shows that there is something missing in their lives. A famous doctor once said that a cure for cancer would be found more quickly than a cure for boredom. Jesus gives people a purpose in life; he gives them strength by which to live; and he gives them peace in which to live. Living with Christ turns mere existence into fullness of life.

(2) It tells us that Jesus is *the restorer of the lost relationship with God*. God sent him to be the atoning sacrifice for sin (verse 10). We do not live in a world in which animal sacrifice is a reality. But we can fully understand what sacrifice meant. When people sinned, the relationship with God was broken; and sacrifice was an expression of penitence, designed to restore that lost relationship. Jesus, by his life and death, made it possible for us to enter into a new relationship of peace and friendship with God. He bridged the awful gulf between us and God.

(3) It tells us that Jesus is *the Saviour of the world* (verse 14). When he came into the world, people were only too well aware of their own weakness and helplessness. As Seneca had it, they were looking *ad salutem*, for salvation. They were desperately conscious of 'their weakness in necessary things'. They wanted 'a hand let down to lift them up'. It would be quite inadequate to think of salvation as mere deliverance

from the punishment of hell. People need to be saved from themselves; they need to be saved from the habits which have become their chains; they need to be saved from their temptations; they need to be saved from their fears and their anxieties; they need to be saved from their follies and mistakes. In every case, Jesus offers salvation; he enables us to face the present and to meet eternity.

(4) It tells us that Jesus is *the Son of God* (verse 15). Whatever that may mean, it certainly means that Jesus Christ is in a relationship to God in which no other person ever stood or ever will stand. He alone can show us what God is like; he alone can bring God's grace, love, forgiveness and strength.

One other thing emerges in this passage. It has taught us about God, and it has taught us about Jesus; and it teaches us about the Spirit. In verse 13, John says it is because we have a share of the Spirit that we know that we dwell in God. It is the work of the Spirit that in the beginning makes us seek God at all; it is the work of the Spirit that makes us aware of God's presence; and it is the work of the Spirit that gives us the certainty that we are truly at peace with God. It is the Spirit in our hearts which makes us dare to address God as Father (Romans 8:15–16). The Spirit is the inner witness who, as C. H. Dodd puts it, gives us the 'immediate, spontaneous, unanalysable awareness of a divine presence in our lives'. Harriet Auber's hymn about the Spirit puts it like this:

> And his that gentle voice we hear,
> Soft as the breath of even,
> That checks each fault, that calms each fear,
> And speaks of heaven.
>
> And every virtue we possess,
> And every victory won,
> And every thought of holiness,
> Are his alone.

LOVE WITHIN THE DIVINE FAMILY

1 John 5:1–2

> Everyone who believes that Jesus is the Christ has
> experienced the birth which comes from God; and
> everyone who loves the father loves the child. This is
> how we know that we must be loving the children of
> God, whenever we love God and keep his command-
> ments.

As John wrote this passage, there were two things in the back
of his mind.

(1) There was the great fact which was the basis of all his
thinking – the fact that love of God and love of others are
inseparable parts of the same experience. In answer to the
questioning scribe, Jesus had said that there were two great
commandments. The first laid it down that we must love
God with all our heart and soul and mind and strength; and
the second laid it down that we must love our neighbour as
ourselves. There are no greater commandments than these
(Mark 12:28–31). John had in mind this word of his Lord.

(2) But he also had in mind a natural law of human life.
Family love is a part of nature. Children naturally love their
parents; and they just as naturally love their brothers and
sisters. The second part of verse 1 means: 'If we love a father,
we also love his child.' John is thinking of the love which
naturally binds us to the parents who gave birth to us and to
the other children whom our parents have brought into the
world.

John transfers this to the realm of Christian thought and
experience. Christians undergo the experience of being reborn;
the father is God; and Christians are bound to love God for all
that he has done for them. But birth is into a family; and

Christians are reborn into the family of God. As it was for Jesus, so it is for them: those who do the will of God, as he himself does, become his mother, his sisters and his brothers (Mark 3:35). If, then, Christians love God the Father who created them, they must also love the other children to whom God is Father. Their love of God and their love of their Christian brothers and sisters must be parts of the same love, so closely interlocked that they can never be separated.

It has been said: 'Man is not only born *to love*, he is also born *to be loved*.' In his commentary, A. E. Brooke put it like this: 'Everyone who has been born of God must love those who have been similarly ennobled.'

Long before this, the psalmist had said: 'God gives the desolate a home to live in' (Psalm 68:6). Christians by virtue of their rebirth are set within the family of God; and as they love the Father, so they must also love the children who are of that same family.

THE NECESSARY OBEDIENCE

1 John 5:3–4a

> For this is the love of God, that we should keep his commandments; and his commandments are not heavy, because everything that is born of God conquers the world.

JOHN reverts to an idea which is never far from the surface of his mind. *Obedience is the only proof of love*. We cannot prove our love to anyone other than by seeking to please and bring joy to that person.

Then, John quite suddenly says a most surprising thing. God's commandments, he says, are not heavy. We must note two general things here.

He certainly does not mean that obedience to God's commandments is easy to achieve. Christian love is no easy matter. It is never an easy thing to love people whom we do not like or people who hurt our feelings or injure us. It is never an easy thing to solve the problem of living together; and, when it becomes the problem of living together according to the Christian standard of life, it is a task of immense difficulty.

Further, there is in this saying an implied contrast. Jesus said of the scribes and Pharisees: 'They tie up heavy burdens, hard to bear, and lay them on the shoulders of others' (Matthew 23:4). The scribal and Pharisaic mass of rules and regulations could be an intolerable burden on the shoulders of any individual. There is no doubt that John is remembering that Jesus said: 'My yoke is easy, and my burden is light' (Matthew 11:30).

How is this to be explained? How can it be said that the tremendous demands of Jesus are not a heavy burden? There are three answers to that question.

(1) It is the way of God never to lay a commandment on anyone without also giving strength to carry it out. With the vision comes the power; with the need for it comes the strength. God does not give us his commandments and then go away and leave us to ourselves. He is there by our side to enable us to carry out what he has commanded. What is impossible for us becomes possible with God.

(2) But there is another great truth here. Our response to God must be the response of love; and, for love, no duty is too hard and no task too great. Things that we would never do for a stranger we will willingly attempt for a loved one. Something that would be an impossible sacrifice, if a stranger demanded it, becomes a willing gift when love needs it.

There is an old story which is a kind of parable of this. Someone once met a young boy going to school long before the days when transport was available. The boy was carrying on his back a smaller boy who was clearly lame and unable to walk. The stranger said to the boy: 'Do you carry him to school every day?' 'Yes,' said the boy. 'That's a heavy burden for you to carry,' said the stranger. 'He's not a burden,' said the boy. 'He's my brother.'

Love turned the burden into no burden at all. It must be so with us and Christ. His commandments are not a burden but a privilege and an opportunity to show our love.

The commandments of Christ are indeed difficult; but burdensome they are not, for Christ never laid a commandment on anyone without giving strength to carry it; and every commandment laid upon us provides another chance to show our love.

We must leave the third answer until our next section.

THE CONQUEST OF THE WORLD

1 John 5:4b–5

> And this is the conquest which has conquered the world, our faith. Who is he who conquers the world but he who believes that Jesus is the Son of God?

(3) We have seen that the commandments of Jesus Christ are not hard to bear because with the commandment there comes the power and because we accept them in love. But there is another great truth. There is something in Christians which makes them able to conquer the world. The *kosmos* is the world apart from God and in opposition to him. The thing that enables us to conquer the *kosmos* is *faith*.

John defines this conquering faith as the belief that Jesus is the Son of God. It is belief in the incarnation. Why should that be able to give us power to overcome? If we believe in the incarnation, it means that we believe that, in Jesus, God entered the world and took our human life upon himself. If he did that, it means that he *cared* enough for us to take upon himself the limitations of humanity, which is the act of a love that is beyond human understanding. If God did that, it means that he *shares* in all the many different activities of human life and knows the many and varied trials and temptations and sorrows of this world. It means that everything that happens to us is fully understood by God and that he is in this business of living along with us. Faith in the incarnation is the conviction that God shares and God cares. Once we possess that faith, certain things follow.

(1) We have a defence to resist the infections of the world. On all sides, there is the pressure of worldly standards and motives; on all sides, there are the fascinations of the wrong things. From within and from outside come the temptations which are part of the human situation in a world and a society not interested in and sometimes hostile to God. But, once we are aware of the constant presence of God in Jesus Christ with us, we have a strong protection against the infections of the world. It is a fact of experience that goodness is easier in the company of good people; and, if we believe in the incarnation, we have the continual presence of God in Jesus Christ.

(2) We have a strength to stand up to the attacks of the world. The human situation is full of things which seek to take our faith away. There are the sorrows and the perplexities of life; there are the disappointments and the frustrations of life; there are, for most of us, the failures and discouragements of life. But, if we believe in the incarnation, we believe in a God who himself went through all this, even to the cross, and who can, therefore, help others who are going through it.

(3) We have the indestructible hope of final victory. The world did its worst to Jesus. It relentlessly pursued him and slandered him. It branded him a heretic and a friend of sinners. It judged him and crucified him and buried him. It did everything humanly possible to eliminate him – *and it failed*. After the cross came the resurrection; after the shame came the glory. That is the Jesus who is with us, one who saw life at its grimmest, to whom life did its worst – who died, who conquered death, and who offers us a share in that victory which was his. If we believe that Jesus is the Son of God, we always have Christ the Victor with us to make us victorious.

THE WATER AND THE BLOOD

I John 5:6–8

> This is he who came through water and blood – Jesus Christ. It was not only by water that he came, but by water and by blood. And it is the Spirit which testifies to this, because the Spirit is truth; because there are three who testify, the Spirit and the water and the blood, and the three agree in one.

THE New Testament scholar A. Plummer, in beginning to comment on this passage, says: 'This is the most perplexing passage in the Epistle, and one of the most perplexing in the New Testament.' No doubt, if we knew the circumstances in which John was writing and had full knowledge of the heresies against which he was defending his people, the meaning would become clear; but, as it is, we can only guess. We do, however, know enough of the background to be fairly sure that we can have some idea of the meaning of John's words.

It is clear that the words *water* and *blood* in connection with Jesus had, for John, a special mystical and symbolic meaning. In his story of the cross, there is a curious pair of verses:

> One of the soldiers pierced his side with a spear, and at once blood and water came out. (He who saw this has testified – so that you also may believe. His testimony is true, and he knows that he tells the truth.)
>
> (John 19:34–5)

Clearly, John attaches particular importance to that incident, and he guarantees it with a very special certificate of evidence. To him, the words *water* and *blood* in connection with Jesus conveyed an essential part of the meaning of the gospel.

The first verse of the passage is rather obscure: 'This is he who came through water and blood – Jesus Christ.' The meaning is that this is the one who entered into his Messiahship or was shown to be the Christ through water and blood.

In connection with Jesus, *water* and *blood* can refer only to two events of his life. The *water* must refer to his *baptism*; the *blood* to his *cross*. John is saying that *both* the baptism and the cross of Jesus are essential parts of his Messiahship. He goes on to say that it was not by water only that he came, but by water *and* by blood. It is, then, clear that some were saying that Jesus came by water, but not by blood; in other words, that his baptism was an essential part of his Messiahship but his cross was not. This is what gives us our clue to what lies behind this passage.

We have seen again and again that behind this letter lies the heresy of Gnosticism. And we have also seen that Gnostics, believing that Spirit was altogether good and matter altogether evil, denied that God came in the flesh. So they had a belief, of which the second-century theologian Irenaeus tells us, connected with the name of Cerinthus, one of the principal representatives of Gnosticism and an exact contemporary of John. Cerinthus taught that, at the baptism, the divine Christ descended into the man Jesus in the form of a dove; Jesus, allied as it were with the Christ who had descended upon him, brought the message of the God who had hitherto been unknown and lived in perfect virtue; then the Christ departed from the man Jesus and returned to glory, and it was only the man Jesus who was crucified on Calvary and afterwards raised from the dead. We might put it more simply by saying that Cerinthus taught that Jesus became divine at the baptism, that divinity left him before the cross and that he died simply a man.

It is clear that such teaching robs the life and death of Jesus of all value for us. By seeking to protect God from contact with human pain, it removes him from the act of redemption.

What John is saying is that the cross is an essential part of the meaning of Jesus and that God was in the death of Jesus every bit as much as he was in his life.

THE TRIPLE WITNESS

1 John 5:6–8 (*contd*)

JOHN goes on to speak of the triple witness.

There is the witness of *the Spirit*. In this, John is thinking of three things. (1) The New Testament story is clear that, at his baptism, the Spirit descended upon Jesus in the most special way (Mark 1:9–11; Matthew 3:16–17; Luke 3:21–2; Acts 10:38; John 1:32–4). (2) The New Testament is also clear that, while John came to baptize with water, Jesus came to baptize with the Spirit (Mark 1:8; Matthew 3:11; Luke 3:16; Acts 1:5, 2:33). He came to bring the Spirit with an abundance and a power previously quite unknown. (3) The history of the early Church is the proof that this was no idle claim. It began at Pentecost (Acts 2:4), and it repeated itself over and over again in the history and experience of the Church (Acts 8:17, 10:44). Jesus had the Spirit, and he could give the Spirit to men and women; and the continuing evidence of the Spirit in the Church was – and is – an undeniable witness to the continuing power of Jesus Christ.

There is the witness of *the water*. At Jesus' own baptism, there was the witness of the Spirit descending upon him. It was, in fact, that event which revealed to John the Baptist who Jesus was. It is John's point that, in the early Church, that witness was maintained in Christian baptism. We must remember that at this early stage in the Church's history, baptism was adult baptism. It was the confession of faith and the reception into the Church of men and women who came directly from the world of Gentile religion and who were beginning an absolutely new way of life. In Christian baptism, things happened. Those who were baptized plunged below the water and died with Christ; they emerged and were raised with Christ to a new life. Therefore, Christian baptism was a witness to the continuing power of Jesus Christ. It was a witness that he was still alive and that he was indeed divine.

There was the witness of *the blood*. The blood was the life. In any sacrifice, the blood was sacred to God and to God alone. The death of Christ was the perfect sacrifice; in the cross, his blood was poured out to God. It was the experience of Christians that that sacrifice redeemed them and reconciled them to God and gave them peace with God. Continuously in the Church, the Lord's Supper, the Eucharist, was and is observed. In it, the sacrifice of Christ is fully displayed; and in it we are given the opportunity not only to give thanks to Christ for his sacrifice made once for all, but also to take for ourselves its benefits and to avail ourselves of its healing power. That happened in John's time. At the Lord's table, people met Christ and experienced his forgiveness and the peace with God which he brings. We still have that experience; and, therefore, that feast is a continuing witness to the atoning power of the sacrifice of Jesus Christ.

The Spirit and the water and the blood all combine to demonstrate the perfect Messiahship, the perfect Sonship and the perfect Saviourhood of this man Jesus in whom was God. The continued gift of the Spirit, the continued death and resurrection of baptism, and the continued availability of the sacrifice of the cross at the Lord's table are still the witnesses to Jesus Christ.

Note on I John 5:7

In the Authorized Version, there is a verse which we have left out. It reads: 'For there are three that bear record in heaven, the Father, the Word and the Holy Ghost; and these three are one.'

The Revised Standard Version omits this verse, and does not even mention it in the margin. (The New Revised Standard Version includes a marginal note on the verse.)

It is quite certain that it does not belong to the original text. The facts are as follows. First, it does not occur in any Greek manuscript earlier than the fourteenth century. The great manuscripts belong to the third and fourth centuries, and it occurs in none of them. None of the great early fathers of the Church knew it. Jerome's original version of the Vulgate, completed early in the fifth century, does not include it. The first person to quote it is a Spanish heretic called Priscillian, who died in AD 385. After that, it crept gradually into the Latin texts of the New Testament, although, as we have seen, it did not gain an entry to the Greek manuscripts.

How did it get into the text? Originally, it must have been an explanation or comment in the margin added by a scribe. Since it seemed to offer good Scriptural evidence for the doctrine of the Trinity, through time it came to be accepted by theologians as part of the text, especially in those early days of scholarship before the great manuscripts were discovered.

But how did it last, and how did it come to be in the Authorized Version? The first Greek testament to be published was that of the Dutch scholar Erasmus in 1516. Erasmus was a great scholar; and, knowing that this verse was not in the original text, he did not include it in his first edition. By this time, however, theologians were using the verse. It had, for instance, been printed in the Latin Vulgate of 1514. Erasmus was therefore criticized for omitting it. His answer was that if anyone could show him a Greek manuscript which had the words in it, he would print them in his next edition. Someone did produce a very late and very bad text in which the verse did occur in Greek; and Erasmus, true to his word, but very much against his judgment and his will, printed the verse in his 1522 edition.

The next step was that, in 1550, Stephanus printed his great edition of the Greek New Testament. This 1550 edition of Stephanus was called – he gave it that name himself – the Received Text, and it was the basis of the Authorized Version and of the Greek text for centuries to come. That is how this verse got into the Authorized Version. There is, of course, nothing wrong with it; but modern scholarship has established that John did not write it and that it is a much later commentary on, and addition to, his words; and that is why all modern translations omit it.

THE UNDENIABLE WITNESS

1 John 5:9–10

> If we accept the testimony of men, the testimony of
> God is greater, for this is the testimony of God that he
> has borne testimony about his Son. He who believes in
> the Son of God has that testimony within himself. He
> who does not believe God has made God a liar, because
> he has not believed in the testimony which God bore to
> his Son.

BEHIND this passage, there are two basic ideas.

There is the Old Testament idea of what constitutes an
adequate witness. The law was quite clear: 'A single witness
shall not suffice to convict a person of any crime or
wrongdoing in connection with any offence that may be
committed. Only on the evidence of two or three witnesses
shall a charge be sustained' (Deuteronomy 19:15; cf. 17:6).
A triple human witness is enough to establish any fact. How
much more must a triple divine witness – the witness of the
Spirit, the water and the blood – be regarded as convincing?

Second, the idea of witness is an integral part of John's
thought. In his gospel, we find different witnesses all
converging on Jesus Christ. John the Baptist is a witness to
Jesus (John 1:15, 1:32–4, 5:33). Jesus' deeds are a witness to
him (John 5:36). The Scriptures are a witness to him (John
5:39). The Father who sent him is a witness to him (John
5:30-2, 5:37, 8:18). The Spirit is a witness to him. 'When the
Advocate comes . . . the Spirit of truth . . . he will testify on
my behalf' (John 15:26).

John goes on to use a phrase which is a favourite of his
in his gospel. He speaks of the person who 'believes in the
Son of God'. There is a wide difference between *believing*

someone and *believing in* that person. If we *believe* someone, we do no more than accept whatever statement that person may be making at the moment as true. If we *believe in* some-one, we accept the whole person and all that that individual stands for in complete trust. We would be prepared not only to trust the spoken word, but also to trust ourselves to that person. To believe in Jesus Christ is not simply to accept what he says as true; it is to commit ourselves into his hands, for time and for eternity.

When we do that, the Holy Spirit within us testifies that we are acting aright. It is the Holy Spirit who gives us the conviction of the ultimate value of Jesus Christ and assures us that we are right to make this act of commitment to him. Those who refuse to do that are refusing the promptings of the Holy Spirit within their hearts.

If people refuse to accept the evidence of those who have experienced what Christ can do, the evidence of the actions of Christ, the evidence of the Scriptures, the evidence of God's Holy Spirit, the evidence of God himself, in effect, they are calling God a liar – and that is the very limit of blasphemy.

THE ESSENCE OF THE FAITH

1 John 5:11–13

> And this is the testimony, that God gave us eternal life and that that life is in his Son. He who has the Son has life; he who has not the Son has not life. I have written these things to you who believe in the name of the Son of God that you may know that you have eternal life.

WITH this paragraph, the letter proper comes to an end. What follows is in the nature of a postscript. The end is a statement that the essence of the Christian life is *eternal life*.

The word for *eternal* is *aiōnios*. It means far more than simply *lasting forever*. A life which lasted forever might well be a curse and not a blessing, an intolerable burden and not a shining gift. There is only one person to whom *aiōnios* may properly be applied, and that is God. In the real sense of the term, it is God alone who possesses and inhabits eternity. *Eternal life* is, therefore, nothing other than *the life of God himself*. What we are promised is that, here and now, there can be given to each one of us a share in the very life of God.

In God, there is *peace*; and, therefore, *eternal life* means *serenity*. It means a life liberated from the fears which haunt the human situation. In God, there is *power*; and, therefore, *eternal life* means *the defeat of frustration*. It means a life filled with the power of God and, therefore, victorious over circumstance. In God, there is *holiness*; and, therefore, *eternal life* means *the defeat of sin*. It means a life clothed with the purity of God and armed against contamination from a wicked world. In God, there is *love*; and, therefore, *eternal life* means *the end of bitterness and hatred*. It means a life which has the love of God in its heart and the undefeatable love of men and women in all its feelings and in all its actions. In God, there is *life*; and, therefore, *eternal life* means *the defeat of death*. It means a life which is indestructible because it has in it the indestructibility of God himself.

It is John's conviction that such a life comes through Jesus Christ and in no other way. Why should that be? If eternal life is the life of God, it means that we can possess that life only when we know God and are enabled to approach him and rest in him. We can do these two things only in Jesus Christ. The Son alone fully knows the Father; and, therefore, only he can fully reveal to us what God is like. As John had it in his gospel, 'No one has ever seen God. It is God the only Son, who is close to the Father's heart, who has made him known' (John 1:18). And Jesus Christ alone can bring us to God. It is in him that the new and living way into the presence of God becomes open to us (Hebrews 10:19–23). We may take a simple analogy. If we wish to meet someone whom we do not know and who moves in a completely different circle from our own, we can achieve that meeting only by finding someone who knows the other person and is willing to introduce us. That is what Jesus does for us in regard to God. Eternal life is the life of God, and we can find that life only through Jesus Christ.

THE BASIS AND THE PRINCIPLE OF PRAYER

1 John 5:14–15

> And this is the confidence that we have towards him, that, if we ask anything which is in accordance with his will, he hears us; and, if we know that he hears anything that we ask, we know that we possess the requests that we have made from him.

HERE are set down both the basis and the principle of prayer.

(1) The *basis of prayer* is the simple fact that God listens to our prayers. The word which John uses for *confidence* is interesting. It is *parrēsia*. Originally, *parrēsia* meant *freedom of speech*, that freedom to speak boldly which exists in a true democracy. Later, it came to mean any kind of confidence. With God, we have freedom of speech. He is always listening, more ready to hear than we are to pray. We never need to force our way into his presence or compel him to pay attention. He is waiting for us to come. We know how we often wait for the post to arrive or for the telephone to ring to bring us a message from someone whom we love. In all reverence, we can say that God is like that with us.

(2) The *principle* of prayer is that, to be answered, it must be *in accordance with the will of God*. Three times in his writings, John lays down what might be called the conditions of prayer. (a) He says that *obedience* is a condition of prayer. We receive whatever we ask because we keep his commandments (1 John 3:22). (b) He says that *remaining in Christ* is a condition of prayer. If we abide in him and his words abide in us, we will ask for anything and it will be done for us (John 15:7). The closer we live to Christ, the more we shall pray aright; and the more we pray aright, the greater the answer we receive. (c) He says that to pray *in his name* is a condition of prayer. If we ask anything in his name, he will do it (John 14:14). The ultimate test of any request is whether we *can* say to Jesus: 'Give me this for *your* sake and in *your* name.'

Prayer must be *in accordance with the will of God*. Jesus teaches us to pray: 'Your will be done,' not 'Your will be changed.' Jesus himself, in the moment of his greatest agony and crisis, prayed: 'Not what I want but what you want . . . Your will be done' (Matthew 26:39, 42). Here is the very essence of prayer. C. H. Dodd writes: 'Prayer rightly considered is not a device for employing the resources of omnipotence to fulfil our own desires, but a means by which our desires may be redirected according to the mind of God, and made into channels for the forces of his will.' A. E. Brooke suggests that John thought of prayer as 'including only requests for knowledge of, and acquiescence in, the will of God'. Even the great Greek and Roman thinkers saw this. The Stoic philosopher Epictetus wrote: 'Have courage to look up to God and say, Deal with me as you will from now on. I am as one with you; I am yours; I flinch from nothing as long as you think that it is good. Lead me where you will; put on me what clothing you will. Would you have me hold office

or refuse it, stay or flee, be rich or poor? For all this I will
defend you before men.'

Here is something on which to ponder. We are so apt to
think that prayer is asking God for what we want, whereas
true prayer is asking God for what he wants. Prayer is not
only talking to God; even more, it is listening to him.

PRAYING FOR THOSE WHO SIN

1 John 5:16–17

> If anyone sees his brother sinning a sin which is not a
> sin whose end is death, he will ask life for him and he
> will give it to him, that is, to those whose sin is not a sin
> whose end is death. There is a sin whose end is death. It
> is not about that that I mean he should ask. All
> wrongdoing is sin; but there is a sin whose end is not
> death.

THERE is no doubt that this is a most difficult and disturbing
passage. Before we approach its problems, let us look at its
certainties.

John has just been speaking about the Christian privilege
of prayer; and now he goes on to single out for special attention the prayer of intercession for someone who needs to be
prayed for. It is very significant that, when John speaks about
one kind of prayer, it is not prayer for ourselves; it is prayer
for others. Prayer must never be selfish; it must never be
concentrated entirely upon our own selves and our own
problems and our own needs. It must be an outgoing activity.
As the New Testament scholar B. F. Westcott put it, 'The end
of prayer is the perfection of the whole Christian body.'

Again and again, the New Testament writers stress the
need for this prayer of intercession. Paul writes to the

Thessalonians: 'Beloved, pray for us' (1 Thessalonians 5:25). The writer to the Hebrews says: 'Pray for us' (Hebrews 13:18). James says that, if any are sick, they ought to call the elders, and the elders should pray over them (James 5:14). It is the advice to Timothy that prayer must be made for everyone (1 Timothy 2:1). Christians have the tremendous privilege of bearing the needs of others to the throne of grace. There are three things to be said about this.

(1) We naturally pray for those who are ill, and we should just as naturally pray for those who are straying away from God. It should be just as natural to pray for the cure of the soul as it is to pray for the cure of the body. It may be that there is nothing greater that we can do for those who are straying away and who are in danger of heading for disaster in their lives than to commit them to the grace of God.

(2) But it must be remembered that, when we have prayed for these people, our task is not yet completed. In this, as in all other things, our first responsibility is to seek to make our own prayers come true. It will often be our duty to speak to them ourselves. We must not only speak to God about them, we must also speak to them about their situation. God needs a channel through which his grace can come and an agent through whom he can act; and it may well be that we are to be his voice in these circumstances.

(3) We have previously thought about the basis of prayer and about the principle of prayer; but here we meet the limitation of prayer. It may well be that God wishes to answer our prayer; it may well be that we pray with heartfelt sincerity; but God's aim and our prayer can be frustrated by those for whom we pray. If we pray for someone who is sick, and that person disobeys the doctors and acts foolishly, our prayer will be frustrated. God may urge, God may plead, God may warn, God may offer; but not even God can violate the

freedom of choice which he himself has given to us. It is often human folly which frustrates our prayers and cancels the grace of God.

SIN WHOSE END IS DEATH

1 John 5:16–17 (*contd*)

THIS passage speaks of the sin whose end is death and the sin whose end is not death. The Revised Standard Version translates it as 'mortal' sin.

There have been many suggestions with regard to this.

The Jews distinguished two kinds of sins. There were the sins which were committed accidentally or, at least, not deliberately. These were sins which might be committed in ignorance, or impulsively, or against the will, in some moment of strong emotion. On the other hand, there were the sins committed out of arrogance, sins deliberately committed out of defiance and in full knowledge that they were against God's will. It was for the first kind of sin that sacrifice atoned; but, for sins of a defiant and arrogant will, no sacrifice could atone.

The scholar A. Plummer lists three suggestions. (1) Mortal sins may be sins which are *punishable* by death. But it is quite clear that more is meant than that. This passage is not thinking of sins which break human laws, however serious. (2) Mortal sins may be sins to which God responds with death. Paul writes to the Corinthians that, because of their unworthy conduct at the table of the Lord, many among them are weak and many are asleep, that is, many have died (1 Corinthians 11:30); and the suggestion is that the reference is to sins which are so serious that God sends death. (3) Mortal sins may be sins punishable with excommunication from the Church. When Paul is writing to the Corinthians about the notorious sinner with whom they have not adequately dealt, he demands that he should be handed over to Satan. That was the phrase for excommunication. But he goes on to say that, serious as this punishment is and terrible as its physical consequence may be, it is designed to save the man's soul in the day of the Lord Jesus (1 Corinthians 5:5). It is a punishment which does not end in death. None of these explanations will do.

There are three further suggestions as to the identification of this mortal sin.

(1) There is a line of thought in the New Testament which points to the fact that some held that there was no forgiveness for sins committed after baptism. There were those who believed that baptism cleansed from all previous sins but that after baptism there was no forgiveness. There is an echo of that line of thought in Hebrews: 'For it is impossible to restore again to repentance those who have once been enlightened, who have tasted the heavenly gift, and have shared in the Holy Spirit, and have tasted the goodness of the word of God and the powers of the age to come, and then have fallen away' (Hebrews 6:4–6). In early Christian terminology, *to be enlightened* was often a technical term for *to be baptized*. It was indeed that belief which made many postpone baptism until the last possible moment. But the real essence of that statement in Hebrews is that restoration becomes impossible when penitence has become impossible; the connection is not so much with baptism as with penitence.

(2) Later on in the early Church, there was a strong line of thought which declared that denial of the faith could never be forgiven. In the days of the great persecutions, some said that those who in fear or in torture had denied their faith could never have forgiveness; for had not Jesus said: 'But whoever denies me before others, I also will deny before my

Father in heaven' (Matthew 10:33; cf. Mark 8:38; Luke 9:26)? But it must always be remembered that the New Testament tells of the terrible denial of Peter and of his gracious restoration. As so often happens, Jesus was gentler and more sympathetic and understanding than his Church was.

(3) It could be argued from this very letter of John that the most deadly of all sins was to deny that Jesus really came in the flesh, for that sin was nothing less than the mark of antichrist (1 John 4:3). If the mortal sin is to be identified with any one sin, that surely must be it. But we think that there is something more to it even than that.

THE ESSENCE OF SIN

1 John 5:16–17 (contd)

First of all, let us try to identify more closely the meaning of the *mortal sin*. In the Greek, it is the sin *pros thanaton*. That means *the sin which is going towards death*, the sin whose end is death, the sin which, if pursued, must result in death. The terrible thing about it is not so much what it is in itself as where it will end if people persist in it.

It is a fact of experience that there are two kinds of sinners. On the one hand, there are those who may be said to sin against their will; they sin because they are swept away by passion or desire, which at the moment is too strong for them. Their sin is a matter not so much of choice as of a compulsion which they are not able to resist. On the other hand, there are those who sin deliberately, on purpose taking their own way, although well aware that it is wrong.

Now, these two types of sinner began by being one and the same. We all know that the first time we do something wrong, we do it with some degree of horror and with fear;

and, after we have done it, we feel grief and remorse and regret. But, if we allow ourselves again and again to flirt with temptation and to fall, on each occasion the sin becomes easier; and, if we think we can escape the consequences, on each occasion the self-disgust and the remorse and the regret become less and less; and in the end we reach a state when we can sin without any qualms at all. It is precisely that which is the sin that is leading to death. As long as people in their heart of hearts hate sin and hate themselves for sinning – as long as they *know* that they are sinning – they are never beyond repentance and, therefore, never beyond forgiveness; but, once they begin to revel in sin and to make it the deliberate policy of their lives, they are on the way to death, for they are on the way to a state where the idea of repentance will not, and cannot, enter their heads.

The mortal sin is the state of those who have listened to sin and refused to listen to God so often that they love sin and regard it as the most profitable thing in the world.

THE THREEFOLD CERTAINTY

1 John 5:18–20

> We know that he who has received his birth from God does not sin, but he whose birth was from God keeps him, and the evil one does not touch him.
>
> We know that it is from God that we draw our being, and the whole world lies in the power of the evil one.
>
> We know that the Son of God has come, and that he has given us discernment to come to know the Real One; and we are in the Real One, even through his Son Jesus Christ. This is the real God and this is eternal life.

JOHN draws to the end of his letter with a statement of the threefold Christian certainty.

(1) Christians are set free from the power of sin. We must be careful to see what this means. It does not mean that Christians never sin; but it does mean that they are not the helpless slaves of sin. As A. Plummer put it, 'A child of God may sin, but his normal condition is resistance to evil.' The difference lies in this. The Gentile world had a deep sense of moral defeat. It knew its own evil and felt there was no possible escape.

The Roman philosopher Seneca spoke of 'our weakness in necessary things'. He said that people 'hate their sins but cannot leave them'. The Roman satirist Persius, in a famous picture, spoke of 'filthy Natta, a man deadened by vice . . . who has no sense of sin, no knowledge of what he is losing, and is sunk so deep that he sends up no bubble to the surface'. The non-Christian world was utterly defeated by sin.

But Christians are men and women who can never lose the battle. Because they are human, they will sin; but they can never experience the absolute moral defeat felt by non-Christians. In his poem 'Saint Paul', F. W. H. Myers makes Paul speak of the battle with the flesh:

> Well, let me sin, but not with my consenting,
>   Well, let me die, but willing to be whole:
> Never, O Christ – so stay me from relenting –
>   Shall there be truce betwixt my flesh and soul.

The reason for the ultimate undefeatedness of Christians is that *he who has his birth from God* keeps them. That is to say, Jesus keeps them. As B. F. Westcott has it, 'The Christian has an active enemy, but he has also a watchful guardian.' Non-Christians are people who have been defeated by sin and have accepted defeat. Christians are people who may sin but never accept the fact of defeat. A saint has been described not as someone who never falls, but as someone who gets up and goes on every time he or she falls.

(2) Christians are on the side of God against the world. The source of our being is God, but the world lies in the power of the evil one. In the early days, the division between the Church and the world was much clearer than it is now. At least in the western world, we live in a civilization permeated by Christian principles. Even if people do not practise them, they still, on the whole, accept the ideals of chastity, mercy, service and love. But the ancient world knew nothing of chastity, and little of mercy, or service, or love. John says that Christians know that they are with God, while the world is in the grip of the evil one. No matter how the situation may have changed, the choice still confronts us whether we will stand with God or with the forces which are against God. As Myers makes Paul say:

> Whoso hath felt the Spirit of the Highest,
> Cannot confound nor doubt him nor deny:
> Yea with one voice, O World, tho' thou deniest,
> Stand thou on that side, for on this am I.

(3) Christians are conscious that they have entered into that reality which is God. Life is full of illusions and impermanencies; by ourselves we can but guess and feel our way, but in Christ we enter into the knowledge of reality. Who am I? What is life? What is God? Where did I come from? Where am I going? What is truth and where is duty? These are the questions to which we can reply only in guesses apart from Jesus Christ. But in Christ we reach the reality, which is God. The time of guessing is gone, and the time of knowing has come.

THE CONSTANT PERIL

1 John 5:21

My dear children, guard yourselves from idols.

WITH this sudden, sharp command, John brings his letter to an end. Short as it is, there is a world of meaning in this phrase.

(1) In Greek, the word *idol* has in it the sense of unreality. Plato used it for the illusions of this world as opposed to the unchangeable realities of eternity. When the prophets spoke of the idols of the Gentiles, they meant that they were false gods, as opposed to the one true God. This may well mean, as Westcott has it, 'Keep yourselves from all objects of false devotion.'

(2) An idol is anything in this life which is worshipped instead of God and allowed to take the place of God. People may make an idol of their money, of their careers, of safety or of pleasure. To quote Westcott again: 'An idol is anything which occupies the place due to God.'

(3) It is likely that John means something more definite than either of these two things. It was in Ephesus that he was writing, and it was of conditions in Ephesus that he was thinking. It is most likely that he means simply and directly: 'Keep yourselves from the pollutions of non-Christian worship.' No town in the world had so many connections with the stories of the ancient gods; and no town was more proud of them. The Roman historian Tacitus writes of Ephesus: 'The Ephesians claimed that Diana and Apollo were not born at Delos, as was commonly supposed; they possessed the Cenchrean stream and the Ortygian grove where Latona, in travail, had reposed against an olive tree, which is still in existence, and had given birth to these deities . . . It was there

that Apollo himself, after slaying the Cyclops, had escaped the wrath of Jupiter: and again that father Bacchus in his victory had spared the suppliant Amazons who had occupied his shrine.'

Further, in Ephesus there stood the great Temple of Diana, one of the wonders of the ancient world. There were at least three things about that Temple which would justify John's stern command to have nothing to do with worship practised there.

(a) The Temple was the centre of immoral rites. The priests were called the *Megabyzi*. They were eunuchs. It was said by some that, in sexual matters, the goddess was so fastidious that she could not bear to have men near her; it was said by others that the goddess was so wanton that it was unsafe for any man to approach her. Heraclitus, the great philosopher, was a native of Ephesus. He was called the weeping philosopher, for he had never been known to smile. He said that the darkness to the approach of the altar of the Temple was the darkness of vileness; that the morals of the Temple were worse than the morals of animals; that the inhabitants of Ephesus were fit only to be drowned, and that the reason that he could never smile was that he lived in the middle of such terrible uncleanness. For a Christian to have any contact with that was to touch infection.

(b) The Temple honoured the right of asylum. Any criminal who could reach the Temple of Diana was safe. The result was that the Temple was frequented by criminals. Tacitus accused Ephesus of protecting crime and calling it the worship of the gods. To have anything to do with the Temple of Diana was to be associated with the very dregs of society.

(c) The Temple of Diana was the centre of the sale of Ephesian letters. These were worn like charms, which were supposed to be effective in bringing about the wishes of those who wore them. Ephesus was 'pre-eminently the city of astrology, sorcery, incantations, amulets [charms], exorcisms, and every form of magical deception'. To have anything to do with the Temple at Ephesus was to be brought into contact with commercialized superstition and black magic.

It is hard for us to imagine how much Ephesus was dominated by the Temple of Diana. It would not be easy for Christians to keep away from idols in a city like that. But John demands that it must be done. Christians must never be lost in the illusions of idolatrous religion; they must never set up in their hearts an idol which will take the place of God; they must keep themselves from the infections of all false faiths; and they can do that only when they walk with Christ.

INTRODUCTION TO THE
SECOND AND THIRD LETTERS OF JOHN

The very shortness of these two letters is the best guarantee of their genuineness. They are so brief and so comparatively unimportant that no one would have gone to the trouble of inventing them and of attaching them to the name of John. A standard papyrus sheet measured ten by eight inches, and the length of these letters is to be explained by the fact that they would each take up almost exactly one sheet.

The Elder

Each of them is said to come from 'the elder' – 2 John begins: 'The elder to the elect lady and her children,' while 3 John begins: 'The elder to the beloved Gaius.' It is extremely unlikely that *the elder* is an official or ecclesiastical title. Elders were officials attached to one congregation whose jurisdiction did not extend outside that congregation, whereas the writer of these letters certainly assumes that he has the right to speak and that his word will carry weight in congregations where he is not actually present. He speaks as one whose authority goes out to the Church at large. The word is *presbuteros*, which originally meant *an elder*, not in the official but in the natural sense of the term. We would be better to translate it as *the ancient*, or *the aged*, for it is not from a position in the Church but from his age and personal qualities that the writer of these letters draws his authority.

In fact, we know that in Ephesus there was a very old man named John who held a very special position. In the days of the early Church, there was a churchman called Papias who lived from about AD 60 to 130. He had a passion for collecting all the information he could lay hands on about the early days of the Church. He was not a great scholar. The fourth-century Church historian Eusebius dismisses him as 'a man of very limited intelligence'; but he does transmit to us some most interesting information. He became Bishop of Hierapolis, but he had a close connection with Ephesus, and he tells us of his own methods of acquiring information. He frequently uses *elder* in the sense of *one of the fathers of the Church*, and he mentions a particularly distinguished *elder* whose name was John. 'I shall not hesitate', he writes, 'to put down for you, along with my own interpretations, whatsoever things I have at any time learned carefully from the *elders*, and carefully remembered, guaranteeing their truth. For I did not, like the multitude, take pleasure in those that speak much, but in those that teach the truth; not in those who relate strange commandments, but in those who deliver the commandments given by the Lord to faith, and springing from the truth itself. If, then, anyone came who had been a follower of the *elders*, I questioned him in regard to the words of the *elders* – what Andrew, or what Peter, had said, or what was said by Philip, or by Thomas, or by James, or by John, or by Matthew, or by any other of the disciples of the Lord; and what things Aristion, or the *Elder John* say. For I did not think that what was to be learned from books would profit me as much as what came from the living and abiding voice.' Clearly, the *Elder John*, John who had reached a great age, was a notable figure in Ephesus, although he is clearly distinguished from John the apostle.

It must be this John who wrote these two little letters. By this time, he was an old man, one of the last surviving links with Jesus and his disciples. He was a man who had the authority of a bishop in Ephesus and in the places around it; and, when he saw that a church was threatened with trouble and heresy, he wrote with gracious and loving correction to his people. Here are the letters of one of the last of the first generation of Christians, a man whom all loved and respected.

Common Authorship

That the two letters are from the one hand there is no doubt. Short as they are, they have a great deal in common. Second John begins: 'The elder to the elect lady and her children, whom I love in the truth.' Third John begins: 'The elder to the beloved Gaius, whom I love in truth.' Second John goes on: 'I was overjoyed to find some of your children walking in the truth' (verse 4); and 3 John goes on: 'I have no greater joy than this, to hear that my children are walking in the truth' (verse 4). Second John comes to an end: 'Although I have much to write to you, I would rather not use paper and ink; instead I hope to come to you and talk with you face to face, so that our joy may be complete' (verse 12). Third John comes to an end: 'I had much to write to you, but I would rather not write with pen and ink; instead I hope to see you soon, and we will talk together face to face' (verses 13–14). There is the closest possible similarity between the two letters.

There is further the closest possible connection between the situation of these letters and that in 1 John. In 1 John 4:3, we read: 'Every spirit that does not confess Jesus is not from God. And this is the spirit of the antichrist, of which you have heard that it is coming; and now it is already in the world.' In 2 John 7, we read: 'Many deceivers have gone out into the world, those who do not confess that Jesus Christ has come in the flesh; any such person is a deceiver and the antichrist.'

It is clear that 2 and 3 John are closely connected with each other, and that both are closely connected with 1 John. They are dealing with the same situation, the same dangers and the same people.

The Problem of the Second Letter

These two little letters confront us with few serious problems. The only real one is to decide whether the Second Letter was sent to an individual or to a church. It begins: 'The elder to the elect lady and her children.' The problem centres on this phrase *the elect lady*. The Greek is *eklektē kuria*, and there are three possible ways of taking it.

(1) It is just possible, though not really likely, that *Eklektē* is a proper name and that *kuria* is a quite usual affectionate address. *Kurios* (the masculine form) has many meanings. It very commonly means *sir*; it means *master* of slaves and *owner* of possessions; on a much higher level, it means *lord* and is the word so often used as a title for Jesus. In letters, *kurios* has a special use. It is practically the equivalent of the English phrase *My Dear*. So, a soldier writes home, saying: *Kurie mou patēr*, My Dear Father. In letters, *kurios* is an address combining affection and respect. It is therefore just possible that this letter is addressed to *My Dear Eklektē*. The biblical scholar Rendel Harris, indeed, went to the lengths of saying that 2 John is nothing other than a Christian love letter. This is unlikely, as we shall see, for more than one reason. But one thing is decisive against it. Second John ends: 'The children of your elect sister send you their greetings.' The Greek is again *eklektē*; and, if it is a proper name at the

beginning of the letter, it must also be a proper name at the end. This would mean that there were two sisters both called by the very unusual name of *Eklektē* – which is simply unbelievable.

(2) It is possible to take *Kuria* as a proper name, for there are examples of this usage. We would then take *eklektē* in its normal New Testament sense; and the letter would be written to the *elect Kuria*. The objections are threefold. (a) It seems unlikely that any single individual could be spoken of as loved by all those who have known the truth (verse 1). (b) Verse 4 says that John rejoiced when he found some of her children walking in the truth; the implication is that others did not walk in the truth. This would seem to imply a number greater than one woman's family could contain. (c) The decisive objection is that, throughout the letter, the *eklektē kuria* is addressed sometimes in the singular and sometimes in the plural. The singular occurs in verses 4, 5 and 13; and the plural occurs in verses 6, 8, 10 and 12. It would be almost impossible that an individual would be addressed in this way.

(3) So, we must come to the conclusion that *the elect lady* means *a church*. There is, in fact, good evidence that the expression was used with this meaning. First Peter, in the Authorized Version, ends with greetings from 'the church that is at Babylon elected together with you' (1 Peter 5:13). The words *church that is* are in italics; that, of course, means that they are not in the Greek and have been supplied in translation to fill out the sense. The Greek literally reads: 'The Elect One at Babylon'; and *The Elect One* is feminine, as is reflected in more modern translations. Few have ever doubted that the phrase means *The church which is at Babylon*; and that is how we must take it in John's letter also. No doubt, the Elect Lady goes back to the idea of the Church

as the Bride of Christ. We can be certain that 2 John is written not to an individual but to a church.

The Problem in the Early Church

Both 2 John and 3 John throw vivid light on a problem which sooner or later had to arise within the organization of the early Church. Let us see if we can reconstruct the situation which lies behind them. It is clear that John, this very old man, regards himself as having a right to act as guide and counsellor and to administer warning and rebuke in the churches whose members are his children. In 2 John, he writes of those who are doing well (verse 4), and by implication suggests that there are others who are not so satisfactory. He further makes it clear that there are travelling teachers in the district, some of whom are preaching false and dangerous doctrine, and he gives orders that such teachers are not to be accepted and not to be given hospitality (verses 7–11). Here, then, John is exercising what is to him an unquestioned right to issue orders to his churches and is seeking to guard against a situation in which travelling teachers of falsehood may arrive at any moment.

The situation behind 3 John is more complicated. The letter is written to one called Gaius, of whose character and actions John most thoroughly approves (verses 3–5). Wandering missionaries have come to the church, people who are fellow helpers of the truth, and Gaius has given them true Christian hospitality (verses 6–8). In the same church is another man called Diotrephes, who loves to put himself first (verse 9). Diotrephes is portrayed as a dictatorial character who will stand no rival to his authority. Diotrephes has refused to receive the wandering teachers of the truth and has actually tried to drive out of the church those who did receive them. He will have nothing to do with travelling teachers even when they are true preachers of the word (verse 10). Then into the picture comes a man called Demetrius, to whom John gives a personal character reference as a good man and one to be hospitably welcomed (verse 12). The simplest explanation of Demetrius is that he must be the leader of a band of wandering teachers who are on their way to the church to which John is writing. Diotrephes will certainly refuse to have anything to do with them and will try to have those who do receive them thrown out; and John is writing to urge Gaius to receive the wandering teachers and not to be intimidated by the domineering Diotrephes, whom he (John) will deal with when he visits the church in question (verse 10). The whole situation turns on the reception of the travelling teachers. Gaius has received such teachers before, and John urges him to receive them and their leader Demetrius again. Diotrephes has shut the door on them and defied the authority of the venerable John.

The Threefold Ministry

All this looks like a very unhappy situation, and indeed it was. Nonetheless, it was one which was bound to arise. In the nature of things, a problem of ministry was bound to emerge within the Church. In its earliest days, the Church had three different kinds of ministries.

(1) Unique, and above all others, stood the *apostles*, those who had been in the company of Jesus and who had been witnesses of the resurrection. They were the undisputed leaders of the Church. Their commission ran throughout the whole Church; in any country and in any congregation, their ministry was supreme.

(2) There were the *prophets*. They were not attached to any one congregation. They were wandering preachers, going where the Spirit moved them and giving to others the message

which the Spirit of God gave to them. They had given up home and occupation and the comfort and the security of a settled life to be the wandering messengers of God. They, too, had a very special place in the Church. The *Didache*, or, to give it its English name, *The Teaching of the Twelve Apostles*, is the earliest book of Church order. In it, the unique position of the prophets is made clear. The order of service for the Eucharist is laid down and the prayers are given; the service ends with the prayer of thanksgiving, which is given in full; and then comes the sentence: 'But suffer the prophets to give thanks as much as they will' (*Didache*, 10:7). The prophets were not to be brought under the rules and regulations which governed ordinary people. So, the Church had two sets of people whose authority was not confined to any one congregation and who had right of entry to every congregation.

(3) There were the *elders*. During their first missionary journey, part of the work of Paul and Barnabas was to ordain elders in all the local churches which they founded (Acts 14:23). The elders were the officials of the settled community; their work was within their congregation, and they did not move outside it. It is clear that they were the backbone of the organization of the early Church; on them the routine work and the solidity of the individual congregations depended.

The Problem of the Wandering Preachers

The position of the apostles presented no real problem; they were unique and their position could never really be disputed. But the wandering prophets did present a problem. Their position was one which was singularly liable to abuse. They had huge prestige; and it was possible for the most undesirable characters to enter into a way of life in which they moved from place to place, living in very considerable comfort at the expense of the local congregations. A clever rogue could make a very comfortable living as a wandering prophet. Even the Greek satirists saw this. The writer, Lucian, in his work called the *Peregrinus*, draws a picture of a man who had found the easiest possible way of making a living without working. He was a trickster who lived off the fat of the land by travelling round the various communities of the Christians, settling down wherever he liked and living luxuriously at their expense. The *Didache* clearly saw this danger and laid down definite regulations to meet it. The regulations are long, but they reveal so much about the life of the early Church that they are worth quoting in full (*Didache*, 11–12).

> If anyone comes and instructs you on the foregoing lines, make him welcome. But should the instructor himself then turn round and introduce teaching of a different and subversive nature, pay no attention to him. If it aims at promoting righteousness and knowledge of the Lord, though, welcome him as you would the Lord.
>
> As regards apostles and prophets, according to the gospel directions this is how you are to act. Every apostle who comes to you should be welcomed as by the Lord, but he is not to stay more than a day, or two days if it is really necessary. If he stays for three days, he is no genuine prophet. And an apostle at his departure should accept nothing but as much provisions as will last him to his next night's lodging. If he asks for money, he is not a genuine prophet.
>
> While a prophet is uttering words in a trance, you are on no account to subject him to any tests or verifications; every sin shall be forgiven, but this sin shall not be forgiven. Nonetheless, not all who speak in trances are prophets unless they also exhibit the manners

and conduct of the Lord. It is by their behaviour that you can tell the impostor from the true. Thus, if a prophet should happen to call out for something to eat while he is in a true trance, he will not actually eat of it; if he does, he is a fraud. Also, even supposing a prophet is sound enough in his teaching, yet if his deeds do not correspond with his words, he is an impostor . . . If any prophet, speaking in a trance, says, 'Give me money (or anything else)', do not listen to him. On the other hand, if he bids you to give it to someone else who is in need, nobody should criticize him.

Everyone who comes 'in the Name of the Lord' is to be made welcome, though later on you must test him and find out about him. You will be able to distinguish the true from the false. If the newcomer is only passing through, give him all the help you can – though he is not able to stay more than a couple of days with you, or three if it is unavoidable. But if he wants to settle down among you, and is a skilled worker, let him find employment and earn his bread. If he knows no trade, use your discretion to make sure that he does not live in idleness simply on the strength of being a Christian. Unless he agrees to this, he is only trying to exploit Christ. You must be on your guard against men of that sort.

The *Didache* even invents the word *Christmonger, trader in Christ, Christemporos*, to describe this kind of person.

John was entirely justified in warning his people that the wrong kind of wandering prophets might come claiming hospitality and in saying that they must on no account be received. There is no doubt that, in the early Church, these wandering prophets became a problem. Some of them were heretical teachers, even if they were sincerely convinced of their own teaching. Some were simply plausible rogues who had found an easy way to make a comfortable living. That is the picture which lies behind 2 John.

The Clash of Ministries

But the situation behind 3 John is in some ways even more serious. The problem figure is Diotrephes. He is the man who will have nothing to do with wandering teachers and who seeks to cast out anyone who dares to give them a welcome. He is the man who will not accept the authority of John and whom John brands as a domineering character. There is much more behind this than meets the eye. This was no storm in a teacup; it was a fundamental split between the local and the travelling ministry.

Obviously, the whole structure of the Church depended on a strong, settled ministry. That is to say, its very existence depended on a strong and authoritative eldership. As time went on, the settled ministry was bound to become frustrated under the remote control of even one so famous and venerable as John, and to resent the possibly upsetting invasions of wandering prophets and evangelists. It was by no means impossible that, however well-intentioned they were, these travellers could do far more harm than good.

Here is the situation behind 3 John. John represents the old apostolic control from a distance; Demetrius and his band of missionaries represent the wandering prophets and preachers; Diotrephes represents the settled ministry of the local elders, who wish to run their own congregation and who regard the wandering preachers as dangerous intruders; Gaius represents the good, well-meaning man who is torn in two and cannot make up his mind.

What happened in this case we do not know. But the end of the matter in the Church was that the wandering preachers faded from the scene, and the apostles in the nature of things passed from this earth, and the settled ministry became the ministry of the Church. In a sense, even in the Church today, the problem of the independent travelling evangelist and the settled ministry is not fully solved; but these two little letters are of the most fascinating interest because they show the organization of the Church in a transitional stage, when the clash between the travelling and the settled ministry was beginning to emerge; and – who knows? – Diotrephes may not have been as bad as he is painted nor altogether wrong.

2 JOHN

THE ELECT LADY

2 John 1–3

> The Elder to the Elect Lady and to her children, whom
> I love in truth (it is not only I who love you and them,
> but so do all who love the truth) because of the truth
> which abides in us and which will be with us forever.
> Grace, mercy and peace will be with us from God the
> Father and from Jesus Christ the Son of the Father, in
> truth and love.

THE writer designates himself simply by the title of the Elder.
Elder can have three different meanings.

(1) It can mean simply *an older man*, one who by reason
of his years and experience is deserving of affection and of
respect. There will be something of that meaning here. The
letter is from someone who has given a long life of service to
Christ and the Church.

(2) In the New Testament, the elders are the *officials of
the local churches*. They were the first of all the church
officials, and Paul ordained elders in his churches on his
missionary journeys as soon as it was possible to do so (Acts
14:21–3). The word cannot be used in that sense here, because
these elders were local officials, whose authority and duties
were confined to their own congregation, whereas the Elder

of this letter clearly has an authority which extends over a much wider area. He claims the right to advise congregations in places where he himself is not a resident.

(3) Almost certainly, this letter was written in Ephesus in the province of Asia. In the church there, *Elder* was used in a special sense. The elders were men who had been direct disciples of the apostles; it is from these men that both Papias and Irenaeus, who lived and worked and wrote in Asia, tell us that they got their information. The elders were the direct links between the second generation of Christians and the followers of Christ during his life on earth. It is un-doubtedly in that sense that the word is used here. The writer of the letter is one of the last direct links with Jesus Christ; and therein lies his right to speak.

As we have already said in the introduction, *the Elect Lady* is something of a problem. There are two suggestions.

(1) There are those who hold that the letter is written to *an individual person*. In Greek, the phrase is *Eklektē Kuria*. *Kurios* (the masculine form of the adjective) is a common form of respectful address, and *Eklektē* could just possibly – though not probably – be a proper name, in which case the letter would be written to *My Dear Eklektē*. *Kuria*, besides being a title of respectful address, can be a proper name, in which case *eklektē* would be an adjective and the letter would be to *the Elect Kuria*. Just possibly, *both* words are proper names, in which case the letter would be to a lady called *Eklektē Kuria*.

But, if this letter is written to an individual, it is much more likely that *neither* word is a proper name and that the Revised Standard Version is correct in translating the phrase as *the elect lady*. There has been much speculation as to who the Elect Lady might be. We mention only two of the sugges-tions. (a) It has been suggested that *the Elect Lady* is Mary, the mother of our Lord. She was to be a mother to John and he was to be a son to her (John 19:26–7), and a personal letter from John might well be a letter to her. (b) *Kurios* means *master*; and *Kuria* as a proper name would mean *mistress*. In Latin, *Domina* has the same meaning; and, in Aramaic, the word is *Martha*; both meaning *Mistress* or *Lady*. It has, therefore, been suggested that the letter was written to Martha of Bethany.

(2) It is much more likely that the letter is written to a *church*. It is far more likely that it is a church which is loved by all who know the truth (verse 1). Verse 4 says that some of the children are walking in the truth. In verses 4, 8, 10 and 12, the word *you* is in the plural, which suggests a church. Peter uses almost exactly the same phrase when he sends greetings from the Elect One (the form is feminine) which is at Babylon (1 Peter 5:13).

It may well be that the address is deliberately unidentifiable. The letter was written at a time when persecution was a real possibility. If it were to fall into the wrong hands, there might well be trouble. And it may be that the letter is addressed in such a way that to the insider its destination is quite clear, while to the outsider it would look like a personal letter from one friend to another.

LOVE AND TRUTH

2 John 1–3 (*contd*)

IT is of great interest to note how in this passage *love* and *truth* are inseparably connected. It is *in the truth* that the elder loves the elect lady. It is *because of the truth* that he loves and writes to the church. In Christianity, we learn two things about love.

(1) Christian truth tells us the way in which we ought to love. *Agapē* is the word for Christian love. *Agapē* is not passion with its ebb and flow, its flicker and its flame; nor is it an easy-going and indulgent sentimentalism. And it is not an easy thing to acquire or a light thing to put into practice. *Agapē* is undefeatable goodwill; it is the attitude towards others which, no matter what they do, will never feel bitterness and will always seek their highest good. There is a love which seeks to possess; there is a love which softens and weakens; there is a love which makes people draw back from a challenge; there is a love which shuts its eyes to faults and to ways which end in ruin. But Christian love will always seek the highest good of others and will accept all the difficulties, all the problems and all the toil which that search involves. It is of significance that John writes in love to warn.

(2) Christian truth tells us the reason for the obligation of love. In his first letter, John clearly sets it down. He has talked of the suffering, sacrificing, incredibly generous love of God; and then he says: 'Beloved, since God loved us so much, we also ought to love one another' (1 John 4:11). *Christians must love because they are loved.* They cannot accept the love of God without showing love to other men and women whom God loves. Because God loves us, we must love others with the same generous and sacrificial love.

Before we leave this passage, we must note one other thing. John begins this letter with a greeting, but it is a very unusual greeting. He says: 'Grace, mercy and peace will be with us.' In every other New Testament letter, the greeting is in the form of a wish or a prayer. Paul usually says: 'Grace be to you and peace.' Peter says: 'May grace and peace be yours in abundance' (1 Peter 1:2). Jude says: 'May mercy, peace, and love be yours in abundance' (Jude 2). But here the greeting is a *statement*: 'Grace, mercy and peace *will be* with us.' John is so sure of the gifts of the grace of God in Jesus Christ that he does not pray that his friends should receive them; he assures them that they will receive them. Here is the faith which never doubts the promises of God in Jesus Christ.

TROUBLE AND CURE

2 John 4–6

> It gave me great joy to find some of your children walking in the truth, as we have received commandment from the Father. And now, Lady, not as if I were writing a new commandment to you, but a commandment which we have had from the beginning, I beg you that we should love one another. And this is love, that we should walk according to his commandments; and this is the commandment, as you have heard from the beginning, that we should walk in it.

In the church to which he is writing, there are things to make John's heart glad and things to make it sad. It brings him joy to know that some of its members are walking in the truth; but that very statement implies that some are not. That is to say, within the church there is division, for there are those who have chosen to walk along different roads. For all things, John has one remedy – and that is love. It is no new remedy and no new commandment; it is the word of Jesus himself: 'I give you a new commandment, that you love one another. Just as I have loved you, you also should love one another. By this everyone will know that you are my disciples, if you have love for one another' (John 13:34–5). Only love can repair a situation in which personal relationships are broken.

Rebuke and criticism are liable to awaken only resentment and hostility; argument and controversy are liable only to widen the split; love is the one thing to heal the break and restore the lost relationship.

But it is possible that those who, as John sees it, have gone the wrong way might say: 'We do indeed love God.' Immediately, John's thoughts go to another saying of Jesus: 'If you love me, you will keep my commandments' (John 14:15). Jesus' actual commandment was to love one another; and, therefore, those who do not keep this commandment do not really love God, however much they may claim to do so. The only proof of our love for God is our love for one another. This is the commandment, says John, which we have heard from the beginning and in which we must walk.

As we go on, we shall see that there is another side to this and that there is no soft sentimentality in John's attitude towards those who were leading people away from the truth; but it is significant that his first cure for all the troubles of the Church is love.

THE THREATENING PERIL

2 John 7–9

> There is all the more reason to speak like this because there have gone out into the world many deceivers, men who do not confess that Jesus is Christ, and his coming in the flesh. Such a man is the deceiver and the antichrist. Look to yourselves that you do not ruin that which we have wrought, but see to it that you receive a full reward. Everyone who advances too far and who does not abide in the teaching of Christ does not possess God; it is he who abides in that teaching who has both the Father and the Son.

ALREADY, in 1 John 4:2, John has dealt with the heretics who deny the reality of the incarnation. There is one difficulty. In 1 John 4:2, the Greek text says that Jesus *has* come in the flesh. The idea is expressed in a participle, and the participle is in the past tense. It is the fact that the incarnation has happened which is stressed. Here, there is a change, and the participle is in the present tense: the literal translation would be that Jesus *comes* or *is coming* in the flesh. As far as the language goes, this could mean either of two things.

(1) It could mean that Jesus is always coming in the flesh, that there is a kind of permanence about the incarnation; that it was not one act which finished in the thirty years during which Jesus was in Palestine, but is timeless. That would be a great thought and would mean that, now and always, Jesus Christ, and God through him, is entering into the human situation and into human life.

(2) It could be a reference to the *second coming*; and it could mean that Jesus is *coming again* in the flesh. It may well be that there was a belief in the early Church that there was to be a second coming of Jesus in the flesh, a kind of incarnation in glory to follow the incarnation of humiliation. That, too, would be a great thought.

But it may well be that the New Testament scholar C. H. Dodd is right when he says that, in a late Greek writer like John, who did not know Greek as the great classical writers knew it, we cannot lay all this stress on tenses, and that it is better to take it that he means the same as he meant in 1 John 4:2. That is, these deceivers are denying the reality of the incarnation and therefore denying that God can fully enter into human life.

It is intensely significant to note how the great thinkers held on with both hands to the reality of the incarnation. In his letters, Ignatius, who was Bishop of Antioch at the beginning of the second century, insists that Jesus was *truly* born, that he *truly* became man, that he *truly* suffered and that he *truly* died. The New Testament scholar Vincent Taylor, in his book *The Person of Christ*, reminds us of two great statements of the incarnation. Martin Luther said of Jesus: 'He ate, drank, slept, waked; was weary, sorrowful, rejoicing; he wept and he laughed; he knew hunger and thirst and sweat; he talked, he toiled, he prayed . . . so that there was no difference between *him* and other men, save only this, that he was *God*, and had no sin.' The German theologian Emil Brunner cites that passage, and then goes on to say: 'The Son of God in whom we are able to believe must be such a One that it is possible to mistake him for an ordinary man.'

If God could enter into life only as a disembodied spirit, it means that the body is always to be despised; then there can be no real communion between the divine and the human; then there can be no real salvation. He had to become what we are to make us what he is.

In verses 8–9, we hear beneath the words of John the claims of the false teachers.

They claim to be *developing* Christianity, discovering more truly what it means. John insists that they are destroying Christianity and wrecking the foundation which has been laid and on which everything must be built.

Verse 9 is interesting and significant. We have translated the first phrase as *everyone who goes too far*. The Greek is *proagōn*. The verb means *to go on ahead*. The false teachers claimed that they were the progressives, the advanced thinkers, the people with open and adventurous minds. John himself was one of the most adventurous thinkers of the New Testament. But he insists that, however far people may advance, they must abide in the teaching of Jesus Christ or they lose touch with God. Here, then, is the great truth.

John is not condemning progressive thinking; but he is saying that Jesus Christ must be the measure of all thinking and that whatever is out of touch with him can never be right. John would say: 'Think – but take your thinking to the touchstone of Jesus Christ and the New Testament picture of him.' Christianity is not a vague, uncontrolled philosophy on the nature of God; it is anchored to the historical figure of Jesus Christ.

NO COMPROMISE

2 John 10–13

> If anyone comes to you and does not bring this teaching, do not receive him into your house and do not greet him on the street; for he who greets him becomes a partner in his evil deeds.
>
> Although I have many things to write to you, I do not wish to do so with paper and ink, but I hope to come to see you and to speak to you face to face, that our joy may be completed.
>
> The children of your Elect Sister send their greetings to you.

HERE, we see very clearly the danger which John saw in these false teachers. They are to be given no hospitality; and the refusal of hospitality would be the most effective way of stopping their work. John goes further; they are not even to be given a greeting on the street. This would be to indicate that to some extent you had sympathy with them. It must be made quite clear to the world that the Church has no tolerance for those whose teaching destroys the faith. This passage may seem on the face of it to imply an attitude which is the exact opposite of Christian love; but the New

Testament scholar C. H. Dodd has certain very wise things to say about it.

It is by no means without parallel. When the saintly Polycarp, the second-century Bishop of Smyrna, met the heretic Marcion, Marcion said: 'Do you recognize me?' 'I recognize Satan's first-born,' answered Polycarp. It was John himself who fled from the public baths when Cerinthus, the heretic, entered them. 'Let us hurry away in case the building should collapse on us,' he said, 'because Cerinthus, the enemy of truth, is here.'

We have to remember the situation. There was a time when it was extremely doubtful whether the Christian faith would be destroyed by the speculations of heretics who preached a false philosophy. Its very existence was in peril. The Church did not dare to risk even appearing to compromise with this destructive corrosion of the faith.

This, as C. H. Dodd points out, is an emergency regulation, and 'emergency regulations make bad law'. We may recognize the necessity of this way of action in the situation in which John and his people found themselves, without in the least holding that we must treat mistaken thinkers in the same way. And yet, to return to Dodd, a good-humoured tolerance can never be enough. 'The problem is to find a way of living with those whose convictions differ from our own upon the most fundamental matters, without either breaking charity or being disloyal to the truth.' It is there that love must find a way. The best way to destroy our enemies, as the American President Abraham Lincoln said, is to make them our friends. We can never compromise with mistaken teachers, but we are never free from the obligation of seeking to lead them into the truth.

So, John comes to an end. He will not write any more, for he hopes to come to see his friends and to speak to them face to face. Both Greek and Hebrew say not *face to face* but *mouth to mouth*. In the Old Testament, the Revised Standard Version tells us that God says of Moses: 'With him I speak mouth to mouth' (Numbers 12:8). John was wise, and he knew that letters can often only bedevil a situation and that five minutes of heart-to-heart talk can do what a whole file of letters is powerless to achieve. In many churches and in many personal relationships, letters have merely succeeded in making a situation worse; for the most carefully written letter can be misinterpreted, when a conversation might have put matters right. The Lord Protector of England, Oliver Cromwell, never understood the Protestant historian John Foxe, and disliked him. Then he met him, and, after he had spoken to him, he said: 'If you and I had but an hour together, we would be better friends than we are.' Church bodies and Christian people would do well to make a resolution never to write when they could speak.

The letter closes with greetings from John's church to the friends to whom he writes – greetings, as it were, from one sister's children to another's, for all Christians are members of one family in the faith.

3 JOHN

THE TEACHER'S JOY

3 John 1–4

> The Elder to Gaius, the beloved, whom I love in truth.
>   Beloved, I pray that everything is going well with
> you, and that you are in good health of body, as it goes
> well with your soul. It gave me great joy when certain
> brothers came and testified of the truth of your life, as
> indeed you do walk in the truth. No news brings me
> greater joy than to hear that my children are walking in
> the truth.

No New Testament letter better shows that the Christian letters
were exactly on the model which all letter-writers used in
the time of the early Church. There is a papyrus letter from a
ship's captain named Irenaeus, to his brother Apolinarius:

> Irenaeus to Apolinarius his brother, my greetings.
> Continually I pray that you may be in health, even as I
> myself am in health. I wish you to know that I arrived
> at land on the 6th of the month Epeiph, and I finished
> unloading my ship on the 18th of the same month, and
> went up to Rome on the 25th of the same month, and
> the place welcomed us, as God willed. Daily we are
> waiting for our discharge, so that up till today no one of
> us in the corn service has been allowed to go. I greet

> your wife much, and Serenus, and all who love you, by
> name. Good bye.

The form of Irenaeus' letter is exactly that of John's. There is
first the greeting, then the prayer for good health, after that
the main body of the letter with its news, and then the final
greetings. The early Christian letters were not something
remote and ecclesiastical; they were the kind of letters which
people wrote to each other every day.

John writes to a friend called Gaius. In the world of the
New Testament, Gaius was the most common of all names.
In the New Testament, there are three men with that name.
There is Gaius the Macedonian, who, along with Aristarchus,
was with Paul at the riot in Ephesus (Acts 19:29). There is
Gaius of Derbe, who was the delegate of his church to convey
the collection for the poor to Jerusalem (Acts 20:4). There is
the Gaius of Corinth who had been Paul's host, and who was
such a hospitable man that he could be called the host of the
whole Church (Romans 16:23), and who was one of the very
few people whom Paul personally had baptized (1 Corinthians
1:14), and who, according to tradition, became the first Bishop
of Thessalonica. Gaius was the most common of all names;
and there is no reason to identify our Gaius with any of these
three. According to tradition, he was made the Bishop of
Pergamum by John himself. Here, he stands before us as a
man with an open house and an open heart.

Twice in the first two verses of this little letter, John uses
the word *beloved*. (The *well-beloved* and *beloved* of the
Authorized Version's first two verses translate the same Greek
word, *agapētos*.) In this group of letters, John uses *agapētos*
no fewer than ten times. This is a very notable fact. These
letters are letters of warning and rebuke; and yet their accent
is the accent of love. It was the advice of a great scholar and

preacher: 'Never scold your congregation.' Even if he has to rebuke, John never speaks with irritation. The whole atmosphere of his writing is that of love.

Verse 2 shows us the comprehensive care of the good and devoted pastor. John is interested both in the physical and the spiritual health of Gaius. John was like Jesus: he never forgot that people have bodies as well as souls and that they matter, too.

In verse 4, John tells us of the teacher's greatest joy. It is to see pupils walking in the truth. The truth is not simply something to be intellectually assimilated; it is the knowledge which fills the mind and the charity which clothes life. The truth is what makes people think and act like God.

CHRISTIAN HOSPITALITY

3 John 5–8

> Beloved, whatever service you render to the brothers, strangers as they are, is an act of true faith and they testify to your love before the Church. It will be a further kindness if you send them on their way worthily of God. For they have gone out for the sake of the Name and they take no assistance from pagans. It is a duty to support such men, that we may show ourselves fellow workers with the truth.

HERE, we come to John's main reason for writing. A group of travelling missionaries is on its way to the church of which Gaius is a member, and John urges him to receive them, to give them every support and to send them on their way in a truly Christian manner.

In the ancient world, hospitality was a sacred duty. Strangers were under the protection of Zeus Xenios, Zeus the god of strangers (*xenos* is the Greek for a *stranger*). In the ancient world, inns were notoriously unsatisfactory. The Greeks had an instinctive dislike of taking money in return for hospitality; and, therefore, the profession of innkeeper was looked down upon. Inns were often dirty and flea-infested. Innkeepers had a reputation for being greedy, so that Plato compared them to pirates who hold their guests to ransom before they allow them to escape. The ancient world had a system of *guest-friendships* whereby families in different parts of the country undertook to give each other's members hospitality when the occasion arose. This connection between families lasted throughout the generations; and, when it was claimed, the claimants brought with them a *sumbolon*, or *token*, which identified them to their hosts. Some cities kept an official called the *Proxenos* in other larger cities to whom their citizens, when travelling, might appeal for shelter and for help.

If the Gentile world accepted the obligation of hospitality, it was only to be expected that the Christians would take it even more seriously. It is Peter's instruction: 'Be hospitable to one another without complaining' (1 Peter 4:9). 'Do not neglect to show hospitality to strangers', says the writer to the Hebrews, and adds: 'for by doing that some have entertained angels without knowing it' (Hebrews 13:2). In the Pastoral Epistles, a widow is to be honoured if she has 'shown hospitality' (1 Timothy 5:10). Paul requests the Romans to 'extend hospitality' (Romans 12:13).

Hospitality was to be especially the characteristic of the leaders of the Church. A bishop must be hospitable (1 Timothy 3:2). Titus is also told to be 'hospitable' (Titus 1:8). When we come down to the time of Justin Martyr (AD 170), we find that on the Lord's Day the wealthy made their contribution and it was the duty of the president of the congregation 'to succour the orphans and the widows, and those who through sickness or any other cause are in want, and those who are in bonds, and the strangers sojourning amongst us' (Justin Martyr, *First Apology*, 1:67).

In the early Church, the Christian home was the place of the open door and the loving welcome. There can be few nobler actions than to give a stranger the right of entry to a Christian home. The Christian family circle should always be wide enough to have a place for strangers, wherever they come from.

THE CHRISTIAN ADVENTURERS

3 John 5-8 (*contd*)

FURTHER, this passage tells us about the wandering missionaries who gave up home and comfort to carry the word of God to other parts. In verse 7, John says that they have gone out for the sake of the Name and that they take no assistance from non-Christians. (It is just possible that verse 7 might refer to those who had come out from the Gentiles taking nothing with them, those who for the sake of Christianity had left their work, their home and their friends and had no means of support.) In the ancient world, the 'begging friar', with his wallet, was well known. There is, for instance, a record of a man calling himself 'the slave of the Syrian goddess', who went out begging and claimed that he never came back with fewer than seventy bags of money for his goddess. But these Christian wandering preachers would take nothing from the Gentiles, even if it had been offered to them.

John commends these adventurers of the faith to the hospitality and the generosity of Gaius. He says that it is a duty to help them so that we may show ourselves fellow workers in the truth (verse 8). James Moffatt translates this very vividly: 'We are bound to support such men to prove ourselves allies of the truth.'

There is a great Christian thought here. Some people's circumstances may be such that they cannot become missionaries or preachers. Life may have put them in a position where they must get on with a secular job, staying in one place and carrying out the routine duties of life and living. But, where they cannot go, their money and their prayers and their practical support can go. Not everyone can be, so to speak, in the front line; but, by supporting those who are there, people can make themselves allies of the truth. When we remember that, all giving to the wider work of Christ and his Church must become not an obligation but a privilege, not a duty but a delight. The Church needs those who will go out with the truth, but it also needs those who will be allies of the truth at home.

LOVE'S APPEAL

3 John 9–15

> I have already written something to the Church, but Diotrephes, who is ambitious for the leadership, does not accept our authority. So, then, when I come, I will bring up the matter of his actions, for he talks nonsensically about us with wicked words; he refuses to receive the brothers and attempts to stop those who wish to do so and tries to eject them from the Church.
>
> Beloved, do not imitate the evil but the good. He who does good has the source of his life in God; he who does evil has not seen God.
>
> Everybody testifies to the worth of Demetrius, and so does the truth itself; and so do we testify, and you know that our testimony is true.

> I have many things to write to you; but I do not wish
> to write to you with ink and pen. I hope to see you
> soon, and we shall talk face to face.
> Peace be to you. The friends send their greetings.
> Greet the friends by name.

HERE, we come to the reason why this letter was written, and
we are introduced to two of the main characters in the story.

There is Diotrephes. In the introduction, we have already
seen the situation in which John, Diotrephes and Demetrius
are all involved. In the early Church, there was a double
ministry. There were the apostles and the prophets whose
area of work was not confined to any one congregation and
whose authority extended all over the Church. There were
also the elders; they were the permanent settled ministry of
the local congregations and their very backbone.

In the early days, this presented no problem, for the local
congregations were still very much infants who had not yet
learned to walk by themselves or to handle their own affairs.
But, as time went on, a tension developed between the two
kinds of ministry. As the local churches became stronger and
more conscious of their identity, they inevitably became less
and less willing to submit to control from a distance or to the
invasion of travelling strangers.

The problem is still to some extent with us. There are
independent travelling evangelists who may well have a
theology and work with methods and in an atmosphere very
different from that of the settled local congregation. In the
younger churches, there may be a question of how long the
missionaries should remain in control and of when the time
has come for them to withdraw and allow the churches of a
particular country to take charge of their own affairs.

In this letter, Diotrephes is the representative of the local
congregation. He will not accept the authority of John, the

apostolic man, and he will not receive the travelling missionaries. He is so determined to see that the local congregation manages its own affairs that he will even expel those who are still prepared to accept the authority of John and to receive the wandering preachers. What exactly Diotrephes' status is, we cannot tell. He is certainly not a bishop in anything like the modern sense of the word. He may be a very strong-minded elder. Or he may even be an aggressive member of the congregation who, by the force of his personality, is sweeping all before him. Certainly, he emerges as a strong and dominant character.

Demetrius is most probably the leader of the wandering preachers and the actual bearer of this letter. John goes out of his way to give him a reference as to character and ability, and it may well be that there are certain circumstances attaching to him which give Diotrephes a handle for his opposition.

Demetrius is by no means an uncommon name. Attempts have been made to identify him with two New Testament characters. He has been identified with Demetrius, the silver-smith of Ephesus and the leader of the opposition to Paul (Acts 19:21ff.). It may be that he afterwards became a Christian and that his early opposition was still held against him. He has been identified with Demas (a shortened form of Demetrius), who had once been one of Paul's fellow workers but who had forsaken him because he loved 'this present world' (Colossians 4:14; Philemon 24; 2 Timothy 4:10). It may be that Demas came back to the faith and that his desertion of Paul was always held against him.

Into this situation come John, whose authority is being flouted, and Gaius – a kindly man but probably not so strong a character as the aggressive Diotrephes – whom John is seeking to get on his side, for, left on his own, Gaius might well give in to Diotrephes.

There is our situation. We may have a good deal of sympathy with Diotrephes; we may well think that he was taking a stand which sooner or later had to be taken. But, for all his strength of character, he had one fault: he was lacking in charity. As the scholar C. H. Dodd has put it, 'There is no real religious experience which does not express itself in charity.' That is why, for all his powers of leadership and for all his dominance of character, Diotrephes was not a real Christian, as John saw it. The true Christian leader must always remember that strength and gentleness must go together and that leading and loving must go hand in hand. Diotrephes was like so many leaders in the Church. He may well have been right, but he took the wrong way to achieve his end, for no amount of strength of mind can take the place of love of heart.

What the outcome of all this was, we do not know. But John comes to the end in love. Soon he will come and talk, when his presence will do what no letter can ever do; and, for the time being, he sends his greetings and his blessing. And we may well believe that the 'Peace be to you' of the Venerable Elder indeed brought calm to the troubled Church to which he wrote.

The Letter of Jude

INTRODUCTION TO
THE LETTER OF JUDE

The Difficult and Neglected Letter

It may well be said that, for the great majority of modern readers, reading the little letter of Jude is a bewildering rather than a profitable undertaking. There are two verses which everyone knows – the resounding and magnificent doxology with which it ends:

> Now to him who is able to keep you from falling and to present you without blemish before the presence of his glory with rejoicing, to the only God our Saviour through Jesus Christ our Lord, be glory, majesty, dominion and authority, before all time and now and forever. Amen.

But, apart from these two great verses, Jude is largely unknown and seldom read. The reason for its difficulty is that it is written out of a background of thought, against the challenge of a situation, in pictures and with quotations, which are all quite strange to us. Without doubt, it would hit those who read it for the first time like a hammer-blow. It would be like a trumpet-call to defend the faith. James Moffatt calls Jude 'a fiery cross to rouse the churches'. But, as J. B. Mayor, one of its greatest editors and commentators, has said, 'To a modern reader it is curious rather than edifying with the exception of the beginning and the end.'

This is one of the main reasons for addressing ourselves to the study of Jude; for, when we understand Jude's thought and disentangle the situation against which he was writing, his letter becomes of great interest for the history of the earliest Church and by no means without relevance for today. There have indeed been times in the history of the Church, and especially in its revivals, when Jude was not far from being the most relevant book in the New Testament. Let us begin by simply setting down the substance of the letter without waiting for the explanations which must follow later.

Meeting the Threat

It had been Jude's intention to write a treatise on the faith which all Christians share; but that task had to be laid aside in view of the emergence of people whose conduct and thought were a threat to the Christian Church (verse 3). In view of this situation, the need was not so much to expound the faith as to rally Christians in its defence. Certain individuals who had insinuated themselves into the Church were busily engaged in turning the grace of God into an excuse for open immorality and were denying the only true God and Jesus Christ the Lord (verse 4). These people were immoral in life and heretical in belief.

The Warnings

Against these intruders, Jude marshals his warnings. Let them remember the fate of the Israelites. They had been brought in safety out of Egypt, but they had never been permitted to enter the promised land because of their lack of belief (verse 5). The reference is to Numbers 13:26–14:29. Despite receiving the grace of God, it was still possible to lose eternal salvation by drifting into disobedience and faithlessness. Some angels with the glory of heaven as their own had come to earth and corrupted mortal women with their lust (Genesis 6:2); and now they were imprisoned in deepest darkness, awaiting judgment (verse 6). Anyone who rebels against God must look for judgment. The cities of Sodom and Gomorrah had given themselves over to lust and to unnatural conduct, and their destruction in flames is a dreadful warning to everyone who similarly goes astray (verse 7).

The Evil Life

These intruders are visionaries of evil dreams; they defile their flesh, and they speak evil of the angels (verse 8). Not even Michael the archangel dared speak evil even of the evil angels. Michael had been given the task of burying the body of Moses. The devil had tried to stop him and claim the body for himself. Michael had spoken no evil against the devil, even in circumstances like that, but had simply said: 'The Lord rebuke you!' (verse 9). Angels must be respected, even when evil and hostile. These evil people condemn everything which they do not understand; and spiritual things are beyond their understanding. They do understand their physical instincts and allow themselves to be governed by them as irrational animals do (verse 10).

They are like Cain, the cynical, selfish murderer; they are like Balaam, whose one desire was for gain and who led the people into sin; they are like Korah, who rebelled against the legitimate authority of Moses and was swallowed up by the earth for his arrogant disobedience (verse 11).

They are like the hidden rocks on which a ship may come to grief; they have their own in-group in which they mix with people like themselves, and thus destroy Christian fellowship; they deceive others with their promises, like clouds which promise the longed-for rain and then pass over the sky; they are like fruitless and rootless trees, which have no harvest of good fruit; as the foaming spray of the waves casts the sea-weed and the wreckage on the beaches, they cast up shameless deeds like foam; they are like disobedient stars which refuse to keep their appointed orbit and are doomed to darkness (verse 13). Long ago, the prophet Enoch had described these people and had prophesied their divine destruction (verses 14–15). They grumble and speak against all true authority and discipline as the children of Israel murmured against Moses in the desert; they are discontented with the lot which God has appointed to them; they are dictated to by their lusts; their speech is arrogant and proud; they pander to and flatter the great for the sake of gain (verse 16).

Words to the Faithful

Having made clear his disapproval of the evil intruders in this torrent of invective, Jude turns to the faithful. They could have expected all this to happen, for the apostles of Jesus Christ had foretold the rise of evil people (verses 18–19). But the duty of all true Christians is to build their lives on the foundation of the most holy faith, to learn to pray in the power of the Holy Spirit, to remember the conditions of the covenant into which the love of God has called them, and to wait for the mercy of Jesus Christ (verses 20–1).

As for the false thinkers and those who indulge in loose living, some of them may be saved with pity while they are still hesitating on the brink of their evil ways; others have to be snatched like pieces of burning wood from the fire; and, in all this rescue work, Christians must have that godly fear which will love the sinner but hate the sin, and must avoid contamination from those they seek to save (verses 22–3).

And, all the time, there will be with them the power of that God who can keep them from falling and can bring them pure and joyful into his presence (verses 24–5).

The Heretics

Who were the heretics whom Jude blasts, what were their beliefs and what was their way of life? Jude never tells us. He was not a theologian but, as James Moffatt says, 'a plain, honest leader of the church'. 'He denounces rather than describes' the heresies he attacks. He does not seek to argue and to refute, for he writes as one 'who knows when round indignation is more telling than argument'. But, from the letter itself, we can deduce three things about these heretics.

(1) They were antinomians – people who believed that the moral law did not apply to them. Antinomians have existed in every age of the Church. They are people who pervert grace. Their position is that the law is dead and they are under grace. The prescriptions of the law may apply to other people, but they no longer apply to them. They can do absolutely what they like. Grace is supreme; it can forgive any sin; the greater the sin, the more the opportunities for grace to abound (Romans 6). The body is of no importance; what matters is the inward heart. All things belong to Christ, and, therefore, all things are theirs. And so, for them, there is nothing forbidden.

So, Jude's heretics turn the grace of God into an excuse for flagrant immorality (verse 4); they even indulge in shameless unnatural conduct, as the people of Sodom did (verse 7). They defile the flesh and do not consider it to be a sin (verse 8). They allow their animal instincts to rule their lives (verse 10). With their sensual ways, they are likely to wreck the Love Feasts of the Church (verse 12). It is by their own lusts that they direct their lives (verse 16).

Modern Examples of the Ancient Heresy

It is a curious and tragic fact of history that the Church has never been entirely free of this antinomianism; and it is natural that it has flourished most in the ages when the wonder of grace was being rediscovered.

It appeared in the Ranters of the seventeenth century. The Ranters were pantheists and antinomians. A pantheist believes that God is everything; literally *all things* are Christ's, and Christ is the end of the law. They talked of 'Christ within them', took no notice of the Church or its ministry, and belittled Scripture. One of them, Jacob Bottomley, in a book entitled *The Light and Dark Sides of God*, wrote: 'It is not safe to go to the Bible to see what others have spoken and written of the mind of God as to see what God speaks within me, and to follow the doctrine and leading of it in me.' When the Quaker George Fox rebuked them for their lewd practices, they answered: 'We are God.' This may sound very fine; but, as John Wesley, the founder of Methodism, was to say, it most often resulted in 'a gospel of the flesh'. It was their argument that 'swearing, adultery, drunkenness and theft are not sinful unless the person guilty of them apprehends them to be so'. When Fox was a prisoner at Charing Cross, they came to see him and greatly offended him by calling for drink and tobacco. They swore terribly and, when Fox rebuked them, justified themselves by saying that Scripture tells us that Abraham, Jacob, Joseph, Moses, the priests and the angel all swore. To this, Fox replied that the one who was before Abraham commanded: 'Swear not at all.' The seventeenth-century Puritan, Richard Baxter, said of them: 'They conjoined a cursed doctrine of libertinism, which brought them to all abominable filthiness of life; they taught . . . that God regardeth not the actions of the outward man, but of the heart; and that to the pure all things are pure (even things forbidden) and so, as allowed by God, they spoke most hideous words of blasphemy, and many of them committed whoredoms commonly . . . The horrid villainies of this sect did speedily extinguish it.' Doubtless, many of the Ranters were insane; doubtless, some of them were pernicious and deliberate pleasure-seekers; but doubtless, too, some of them were earnest but misguided people who had misunderstood the meaning of grace and freedom from the law.

Later, John Wesley was to have trouble with the antinomians. He talks of them preaching a gospel of flesh and blood. At Jenninghall, he says that 'the antinomians had laboured hard in the Devil's service'. At Birmingham, he says that 'the fierce, unclean, brutish, blasphemous antinomians' had utterly destroyed the spiritual life of the congregation. He tells of a certain Roger Ball who worked his way into the life of the congregation at Dublin. At first, he seemed to be so spiritually minded that the congregation welcomed him as being well suited for the service and ministry of the Church. He showed himself in time to be 'full of guile and of the most abominable errors, one of which was that a believer had a right to all women'. He would not take communion, for under grace a man must 'touch not, taste not, handle not'. He would not preach, and abandoned the church services because, he said, 'The dear Lamb is the only preacher.'

Wesley, deliberately to show the position of these antinomians, related in his *Journal* a conversation which he had with one of them at Birmingham. It ran as follows. 'Do you believe that you have nothing to do with the law of God?' 'I have not; I am not under the law; I live by faith.' 'Have you, as living by faith, a right to everything in the world?' 'I have. All is mine, since Christ is mine.' 'May you then take anything you will anywhere? Suppose out of a shop without the consent or knowledge of the owner?' 'I may, if I want, for it is mine. Only I will not give offence.' 'Have you a right to all the women in the world?' 'Yes, if they consent.' 'And is not that a sin?' 'Yes, to him who thinks it is a sin; but not to those whose hearts are free.'

Repeatedly, Wesley had to meet these people, as George Fox had to meet them. John Bunyan, too, came up against the Ranters, who claimed complete freedom from the moral law and looked with contempt on the ethics of stricter Christians. 'These would condemn me as legal and dark, pretending that they only had attained perfection that could do what they would and not sin.' One of them, whom Bunyan knew, 'gave himself up to all manner of filthiness, especially uncleanness . . . and would laugh at all exhortations to sobriety. When I laboured to rebuke his wickedness, he would laugh the more.'

Jude's heretics have existed in every Christian generation; and, even if they do not go all the way, there are still many who in their heart of hearts trade upon God's forgiveness and make his grace an excuse to sin.

The Denial of God and of Jesus Christ

(2) Of the antinomianism and blatant immorality of the heretics whom Jude condemns, there is no doubt. The other two faults with which he charges them are not so obvious in their meaning. He charges them with, as the Revised Standard Version has it, 'denying our only Master and Lord, Jesus Christ' (verse 4). The closing doxology is to 'the only God', a phrase which occurs again in Romans 16:27 and 1 Timothy 1:17 (cf. 1 Timothy 6:15). The reiteration of the word *only* is significant. If Jude talks about our *only* Master and Lord and about the *only* God, it is natural to assume that there must have been those who questioned the uniqueness of Jesus Christ and of God. Can we trace any such line of thought in the early Church; and, if so, does it fit in with any other evidence which may be supplied by hints within the letter itself?

As so often in the New Testament, we are again in contact with that type of thought which came to be known as Gnosticism. Its basic idea was that this was a dualistic universe, a universe with two eternal principles in it. From the beginning of time, there had always been spirit and matter. Spirit was essentially good; matter was essentially evil. Out of this flawed matter, the world was created. Now, God is pure spirit and, therefore, could not possibly have contact with matter because it was essentially evil. How then was creation brought about? God put out a series of aeons or divine powers; each of these aeons was further away from him. At the end of this long chain, remote from God, there was an aeon who was able to touch matter; and it was this aeon, this distant and secondary god, who actually created the world.

Nor was this all that was in Gnostic thought. As the aeons in the series grew more distant from God, they grew more ignorant of him – and also grew more hostile to him. The creating aeon, at the end of the series, was both totally ignorant of and totally hostile to God.

Having gone that far, the Gnostics took another step. They identified the true God with the God of the New Testament, and they identified the secondary, ignorant and hostile god with the God of the Old Testament. As they saw it, the God of creation was a different being from the God of revelation and redemption. Christianity, on the other hand, believes in the *only* God, the one God of creation, providence and redemption.

This was the Gnostic explanation of sin. It was because creation was carried out, in the first place, from evil matter and, in the second place, by an ignorant god, that sin and suffering and all imperfection existed.

This Gnostic line of thought had one curious but perfectly logical result. If the God of the Old Testament was ignorant of and hostile to the true God, it must follow that the people whom that ignorant God hurt were in fact *good* people. Clearly, the hostile God would be hostile to the people who were the true servants of the true God. The Gnostics, therefore, so to speak, turned the Old Testament upside down and regarded its heroes as villains and its villains as heroes. So, there was a sect of these Gnostics called Ophites, because they worshipped the serpent of Eden (the Greek word for snake is *ophis*); and there were those who regarded Cain and Korah and Balaam as great heroes. It is these very people whom Jude uses as tragic and terrible examples of sin.

So, we may take it that the heretics whom Jude attacks are Gnostics who denied the oneness of God, who regarded the God of creation as different from the God of redemption, who saw in the Old Testament God an ignorant enemy of the true God and who, therefore, turned the Old Testament upside down to regard its sinners as servants of the true God and its saints as servants of the hostile God.

Not only did these heretics deny the oneness of God, they also denied 'our only Master and Lord Jesus Christ'. That is to say, they denied the uniqueness of Jesus Christ. How does that fit in with the Gnostic ideas as far as they are known to us? We have seen that, according to Gnostic belief, God put out a series of aeons between himself and the world. The Gnostics regarded Jesus Christ as one of these aeons. They did not regard him as our *only* Master and Lord; he was only one among the many who were links between God and human beings, although he might be the highest and the closest of all.

There is still one other hint about these heretics in Jude, a hint which also fits in with what we know about the Gnostics. In verse 19, Jude describes them as 'these who set up divisions'. The heretics introduce some kind of class distinctions within the fellowship of the Church. What were these distinctions?

We have seen that, between human beings and God, there stretched an infinite series of aeons. The aim of men and women must be to achieve contact with God. To obtain this, their souls must cross this infinite series of links between themselves and God. The Gnostics held that, to achieve this, a very special and secret knowledge was required. So deep was this knowledge that only very few could attain to it.

The Gnostics, therefore, divided people into two classes – the *pneumatikoi* and the *psuchikoi*. The *pneuma* was the human spirit, that which made human beings kin to God; and the *pneumatikoi* were the *spiritual* people, the people whose spirits were so highly developed and intellectual that they were able to climb the long ladder and reach God. These *pneumatikoi*, the Gnostics claimed, were so spiritually and intellectually equipped that they could become as good as Jesus. Irenaeus, the second-century Bishop of Lyons, says that some of them believed that the *pneumatikoi* could become *better* than Jesus and attain direct union with God.

On the other hand, the *psuchē* was simply the principle of physical life. All things which lived had *psuchē*; it was something which human beings shared with the animal creation and even with growing plants. The *psuchikoi* were ordinary people; they had physical life, but their *pneuma* was undeveloped, and they were incapable of ever gaining the intellectual wisdom which would enable them to climb the long road to God. The *pneumatikoi* were a very small and select minority; the *psuchikoi* were the vast majority of ordinary people.

It is clear that this kind of belief inevitably produced spiritual snobbery and pride. It introduced into the Church the worst kind of class distinction.

So, the heretics whom Jude attacks were people who denied the oneness of God and split him into an ignorant creating God and a truly spiritual God. They denied the uniqueness of Jesus Christ and saw him as only one of the links between God and human beings, and they created class distinctions within the Church and limited fellowship with God to the intellectual few.

The Denial of the Angels

(3) It is further implied that these heretics denied and insulted the angels. It is said they 'reject authority, and revile the glorious ones' (verse 8). The words 'authority' and 'glorious ones' describe ranks in the Jewish hierarchy of angels. Verse 9 is a reference to a story in *The Assumption of Moses* (see above, page 181). If Michael, the archangel, on such an occasion said nothing against the prince of evil angels, clearly no one can speak evil of the angels.

The Jewish belief in angels was very elaborate. Every nation had a protecting angel. Every person, even every child, had an angel. All the forces of nature, the wind and the sea and the fire and all the others, were under the control of angels. It could even be said: 'Every blade of grass has its angel.' Clearly, the heretics attacked the angels. It is likely that they said that the angels were the servants of the ignorant and hostile creator God and that Christians must have nothing to do with them. We cannot quite be sure what lies behind this; but, to all their other errors, the heretics added the despising of the angels, and to Jude this seemed an evil thing.

Jude and the New Testament

We must now examine the questions regarding the date and the authorship of Jude.

Jude had some difficulty in getting into the New Testament at all; it is one of the books whose position was always insecure and which were late in gaining full acceptance as part of the New Testament. Let us briefly set out the opinions of the great fathers and scholars of the early Church about it.

Jude is included in the Muratorian Canon, which dates to about AD 170 and may be regarded as the first semi-official list of the books accepted by the Church. The inclusion of Jude is strange when we remember that the Muratorian Canon does not include in its list Hebrews and 1 Peter. But, for a long time thereafter, Jude is spoken of with some doubt. In the middle of the third century, the biblical scholar Origen knew and used it, but he was well aware that there were many who questioned its right to be Scripture. Eusebius, the great scholar of the middle of the fourth century, made a deliberate examination of the position of the various books which were in use, and he classed Jude among the books which were disputed.

Jerome, who completed the Latin version of the Bible, the Vulgate, in the early years of the fifth century, had his doubts about Jude; and it is in him that we find one of the reasons for the hesitation which was felt towards it. The strange thing about Jude is the way in which it quotes as authorities books which are *outside* the Old Testament. It uses as Scripture certain books which were written between the Old and the New Testaments and were never generally regarded as Scripture. Here are two definite instances. The reference in verse 9 to Michael arguing with the devil about the body of Moses is taken from an apocryphal book called *The Assumption of Moses*. In verses 14–15, Jude confirms his argument with a quotation from prophecy, as, indeed, is the habit of all the New Testament writers; but Jude's quotation is, in fact, taken from the Book of Enoch, which he appears to regard as Scripture. Jerome tells us that it was Jude's habit of using non-Scriptural books as Scripture which made some people regard him with suspicion; and, towards the end of the third century in Alexandria, it was from the very same charge that the blind theologian Didymus defended him. It is perhaps the strangest thing in Jude that he uses these non-Scriptural books as other New Testament writers use the prophets; and in verses 17–18 he makes use of a saying of the apostles which is not identifiable at all.

Jude, then, was one of the books which took a long time to gain an assured place in the New Testament; but, by the fourth century, its place was secure.

The Date

There are definite indications that Jude is not an early book. It speaks of the faith that was once delivered to the saints (verse 3). That way of speaking seems to look back a long way and to come from the time when there was a body of belief that was orthodoxy. In verses 17–18, he urges his people to remember the words of the apostles of the Lord Jesus Christ. That seems to come from a time when the apostles were no longer there and the Church was looking back on their teaching. The atmosphere of Jude is of a book which looks back.

Beside that, we have to set the fact that, as it seems to us, 2 Peter makes use of Jude to a very large extent. Anyone can see that its second chapter has the closest possible connection with Jude. It is quite certain that one of these writers was borrowing from the other. On general grounds, it is much more likely that the author of 2 Peter would incorporate the whole of Jude into his work than that Jude would, for no apparent reason, take over only one section of 2 Peter. Now, if we believe that 2 Peter uses it, Jude cannot be very late, even if it is not early.

It is true that Jude looks back on the apostles; but it is also true that, with the exception of John, all the apostles were dead by AD 70. Taking together the fact that Jude looks back on the apostles and the fact that 2 Peter uses it, a date about AD 80–90 would suit the writing of Jude.

The Authorship of Jude

Who was the Jude, or Judas, who wrote this letter? He calls himself the servant of Jesus Christ and the brother of James. In the New Testament, there are five people called Judas.

(1) There is the Judas of Damascus in whose house Paul was praying after his conversion on the Damascus road (Acts 9:11).

(2) There is Judas Barsabas, a leading figure in the councils of the Church, who, along with Silas, was the bearer to Antioch of the decision of the Council of Jerusalem when the door of the Church was opened to the Gentiles (Acts 15:22, 27, 32). This Judas was also a prophet (Acts 15:32).

(3) There is Judas Iscariot.

None of these three has ever been considered seriously as the author of this letter.

(4) There is the second Judas in the apostolic band. John calls him Judas, not Iscariot (John 14:22). In Luke's list of the Twelve, there is an apostle whom the Authorized Version calls Judas *the brother* of James (Luke 6:16; Acts 1:13). If we were to depend solely on the Authorized Version, we might well think that here we have a serious candidate for the authorship of this letter; and, indeed, the Church father Tertullian calls the writer the Apostle Judas. But, in the Greek, this man is simply called *Judas of James*. This is a very common idiom in Greek, and almost always it means not

brother of but *son of* – so that *Judas of James* in the list of the Twelve is not Judas the *brother* of James but Judas the *son* of James, as all the more modern translations show.

(5) There is the Judas who was the brother of Jesus (Matthew 13:55; Mark 6:3). If any of the New Testament Judases is the writer of this letter, it must be this one, for only he could truly be called *the brother of James*.

Is this little letter to be taken as a letter of the Judas who was the brother of our Lord? If so, it would give it a special interest. But there are objections.

(1) If Jude – to use the form of his name with which we are familiar – was the brother of Jesus, why does he not say so? Why does he identify himself as Jude the brother of James rather than as Jude the brother of Jesus? It would surely be explanation enough to say that he shrank from taking so great a title of honour to himself. Even if it was true that he was the brother of Jesus, he might well prefer in humility to call himself his servant, for Jesus was not only his brother but also his Lord. Further, Jude the brother of James would in all probability never have gone outside Palestine in all his life. The church he would know would be the one in Jerusalem, and of that church James was the undoubted head. If he was writing to churches in Palestine, his relationship to James was the natural thing to stress. When we come to think of it, it would be more surprising that Jude should call himself the brother of Jesus than that he should call himself the servant of Jesus Christ.

(2) The objection is raised that Jude calls himself the servant of Jesus Christ and thereby calls himself an apostle. 'Servants of God' was the Old Testament title for the prophets. God would not do anything without revealing it first to his servants the prophets (Amos 3:7). What had been a prophetic title in the Old Testament became an apostolic title in the

New Testament. Paul speaks of himself as the servant of Jesus Christ (Romans 1:1; Philippians 1:1). In the Pastoral Epistles, he is spoken of as the servant of God (Titus 1:1), and that is also the title which James takes for himself (James 1:1). The conclusion is reached, therefore, that by calling himself 'the servant of Jesus Christ' Jude is claiming to be an apostle.

There are two answers to that. First, the title of servant of Jesus Christ is not confined to the Twelve, for it is given by Paul to Timothy (Philippians 1:1). Second, even if it is regarded as a title confined to the apostles in the wider sense of the word, we find the brothers of the Lord associated with the eleven after the ascension (Acts 1:14), and Jude, like James, may well have been among them; and we learn that the brothers of Jesus were prominent in the missionary work of the Church (1 Corinthians 9:5). Such evidence as we have would tend to prove that Jude, the brother of our Lord, was one of the apostolic circle and that the title of servant of Jesus Christ is perfectly applicable to him.

(3) It is argued that the Jude of Palestine, who was the brother of Jesus, could not have written the Greek of this letter, as he would have been an Aramaic-speaker. That is not a safe argument. Jude would certainly know Greek, for it was the common language of the ancient world, which people spoke in addition to their own language. The Greek of Jude is unrefined and forceful. It might well have been within Jude's competence to write it for himself; and, even if he could not do so, he may well have had a helper and translator such as Peter had in Silvanus.

(4) It might be argued that the heresy which Jude is attacking is Gnosticism, and that Gnosticism is much more a Greek than a Jewish way of thought – and what would Jude of Palestine be doing writing to Greeks? But an odd fact about this heresy is that it is the very opposite of orthodox Judaism.

All Jewish action was controlled by sacred law; the first basic belief of Judaism was that there was one God, and the Jewish belief in angels was highly developed. It is by no means difficult to suppose that, when certain Jews entered the Christian faith, they swung to the other extreme. It is easy to imagine Jews, who all their lives had been slaves to the law, suddenly discovering grace and plunging into antinomianism as a reaction against their former legalism, and reacting similarly against the traditional Jewish belief in one God and in angels. In the heretics whom Jude attacks, it is in fact easy to see Jews who had come into the Christian Church more as deserters from Judaism than as truly convinced Christians.

(5) Last, it might be argued that, if this letter had been known to have been the work of Jude the brother of Jesus, it would not have been so long in gaining an entry into the New Testament. But, before the end of the first century, the Church was largely Gentile, and the Jews were regarded as the enemies and the slanderers of the Church. During his lifetime, Jesus' brothers had in fact been his enemies; and it could well have happened that a letter as Jewish as Jude might have had a struggle against prejudice to get into the New Testament, even if its author was the brother of Jesus.

Jude the Brother of Jesus

If this letter is not the work of Jude the brother of Jesus, what are the alternative suggestions? There are two.

(1) The letter is the work of a man called Jude of whom nothing is otherwise known. This theory has to meet a double difficulty. First, there is the coincidence that this Jude is also the brother of James. Second, it is hard to explain how so small a letter ever came to have any authority at all, if it is the work of someone quite unknown.

(2) The letter is pseudonymous. That is to say, it was written by someone else and then attached to the name of Jude. That was a common practice in the ancient world. Between the Old and the New Testament, scores of books were written and attached to the names of Moses, Enoch, Baruch, Isaiah, Solomon and many others. No one saw anything wrong in that. But two things are to be noted about Jude.

(a) In all such publications, the name to which the book was attached was a famous name; but Jude, the brother of our Lord, was a person who was completely obscure; he is not numbered among the great names of the early Church. There is a story that, in the days of the Emperor Domitian, there was a deliberate attempt to see to it that Christianity did not spread. News came to the Roman authorities that certain descendants from the family of Jesus were still alive, among them the grandsons of Jude. The Romans felt that it was possible that rebellion might gather around these men, and they were ordered to appear before the Roman courts. When they did so, they were seen to be labourers and land workers and were dismissed as being unimportant and quite harmless. Obviously, Jude was Jude the obscure, and there could have been no possible reason for attaching a book to the name of a man whom nobody knew.

(b) When a book was written under a pseudonym, the reader was never left in any doubt as to the person whose name it was being attached to. If this letter had been issued as the work of Judas the brother of our Lord, he would certainly have been given that title in such a way that no one could mistake it; and yet, in fact, it is quite unclear who the author is.

Jude is obviously Jewish; its references and allusions are such that only a Jew could understand them. It is simple and unrefined; it is vivid and pictorial. It is clearly not the work of a theologian. It fits Jude the brother of our Lord. It is attached to his name, and there could be no reason for doing that unless he did in fact write it.

It is our opinion that this little letter is actually the work of Judas, the brother of Jesus.

JUDE

WHAT IT MEANS TO BE A CHRISTIAN

Jude 1–2

> Jude, the servant of Jesus Christ and the brother of
> James, sends this letter to the called who are beloved in
> God and kept by Jesus Christ. May mercy and peace
> and love be multiplied to you.

Few things tell more about people than the way in which they speak about themselves; few things are more revealing than the titles by which they wish to be known. Jude calls himself the servant of Jesus Christ and the brother of James. Immediately, this tells us two things about him.

(1) Jude was a man happy to take second place. He was not nearly so well known as James; and he is content to be known as the *brother of James*. In this, he was the same as Andrew. Andrew was Simon Peter's brother (John 6:8). He, too, was described by his relationship to a more famous brother. Jude and Andrew might well have been resentful of the brothers in whose shadow they had to live; but both had the great gift of gladly taking second place.

(2) The only title of honour which Jude would allow himself was *the servant of Jesus Christ*. The Greek is *doulos*, and it means more than *servant* – it means *slave*. That is to

say, Jude regarded himself as having only one purpose and one distinction in life – to be forever at the disposal of Jesus for service in his cause. The greatest glory which any Christian can attain is to be of use to Jesus Christ.

In this introduction, Jude uses three words to describe Christians.

(1) Christians are those who are *called by God*. The Greek for *to call* is *kalein*; and *kalein* has three great areas of use.

(a) It is the word for summoning a person to *office*, to *duty* and to *responsibility*. Christians are summoned to a task, to duty and to responsibility in the service of Christ.

(b) It is the word for summoning someone to a *feast* or a *festival*. It is the word for an invitation to a happy occasion. Christians are people who are summoned to the joy of being the guests of God.

(c) It is the word for summoning a person to *judgment*. It is the word for calling people to court to give account of themselves. Christians are in the end summoned to appear before the judgment seat of Christ.

(2) Christians are those who are *beloved in God*. It is this great fact which determines the nature of the call. The call to men and women is the call to be loved and to love. God calls us to a task; but that task is an honour, not a burden. God calls us to service; but it is the service of fellowship, not of tyranny. In the end, God calls us to judgment; but it is the judgment of love as well as of justice.

(3) Christians are those who are *kept by Christ*. As Christians we are never left alone; Christ is always watching over our lives, and he is our companion on the way.

THE CALL OF GOD

Jude 1-2 (*contd*)

BEFORE we leave this opening passage, let us think a little more about this calling of God and try to see something of what it means.

(1) Paul speaks about being called to be an *apostle* (Romans 1:1; 1 Corinthians 1:1). In Greek, the word is *apostolos*; it comes from the verb *apostellein, to send out*, and an apostle is, therefore, *one who is sent out*. That is to say, Christians are the ambassadors of Christ. They are sent out into the world to speak for Christ, to act for Christ and to live for Christ. By their lives, they commend, or fail to commend, Christ to others.

(2) Paul speaks about being called to be *saints* (Romans 1:7; 1 Corinthians 1:2). The word for *saint* is *hagios*, which is also very commonly translated as *holy*. Its root idea is *difference*. The Sabbath is holy because it is different from other days; God is supremely holy because he is different from us. To be called to be a *saint* is to be called to be *different*. The world has its own standards and its own scale of values. The difference for Christians is that Christ is the only standard and loyalty to Christ the only value.

(3) Christians are called *according to the purpose of God* (Romans 8:28). God's call goes out to everyone, although not everyone accepts it; and this means that, for every individual, God has a purpose. Christians are men and women who submit themselves to the purpose God has for them.

Paul has a good deal to say about this calling of God, and we can set it down only very briefly. It sets before us a great hope (Ephesians 1:18, 4:4). It should be a unifying influence binding people together by the conviction that they all have a part in the purpose of God (Ephesians 4:4). It is an *upward* calling (Philippians 3:14), setting our feet on the way to the stars. It is a *heavenly* calling (Hebrews 3:1), making us think of the things which are invisible and eternal. It is a *holy* calling, a call to consecration to God. It is a calling which covers ordinary everyday tasks (1 Corinthians 7:20). It is a calling which does not alter, because God does not change his mind (Romans 11:29). It knows no human distinctions and cuts across the world's classifications and judgments (1 Corinthians 1:26). It is something of which Christians must be worthy (Ephesians 4:1; 2 Thessalonians 1:11); and all life must be one long effort to make it secure (2 Peter 1:10).

The calling of God is the privilege, the challenge and the inspiration of the Christian life.

DEFENDING THE FAITH

Jude 3

> Beloved, when I was in the midst of devoting all my energy to writing to you about the faith which we all share, I felt that I was compelled to write a letter to you to urge you to engage upon the struggle to defend the faith which was once and for all delivered to God's consecrated people.

HERE, we have the occasion which prompted the letter. Jude had been engaged on writing a treatise about the Christian faith; but news had come that evil and misguided people had been spreading destructive teaching. He became convinced that he must lay aside his treatise and write this letter.

Jude fully realized his duty to be the watchman of God's flock. The purity of their faith was threatened, and he rushed to defend both them and the faith. That involved setting aside the work on which he had been engaged; but often it is much better to write a tract for the times than a treatise for the future. It may be that Jude never again got the chance to write the treatise he had planned; but the fact is that he did more for the Church by writing this urgent little letter than he could possibly have done by leaving a long treatise on the faith.

In this passage, there are certain truths about the faith which we hold.

(1) The faith is *something which is delivered to us*. The facts of the Christian faith are not something which we have discovered for ourselves. In the true sense of the word, they are *tradition*, something which has been handed down from generation to generation until it has come to us. They go back in an unbroken chain to Jesus Christ himself.

There is something to be added to that. The facts of the faith are indeed something which we have not discovered for ourselves. It is, therefore, true that the Christian tradition is not something handed down in the cold print of books; it is something which is passed on from person to person through the generations. The chain of Christian tradition is a living chain whose links are men and women who have experienced the wonder of the facts.

(2) The Christian faith is *something which is once and for all delivered to us*. There is in it an unchangeable quality. That is not to say that every age does not have to rediscover the Christian faith; but it does say that there is an unchanging nucleus in it – and the permanent centre of it is that Jesus Christ came into the world and lived and died to bring salvation to men and women.

(3) The Christian faith is *something which is entrusted to God's consecrated people*. That is to say, the Christian faith is the possession not of any one person but of the Church. It

comes down within the Church, it is preserved within the Church and it is understood within the Church.

(4) The Christian faith is *something which must be defended*. Every Christian must be its defender. If the Christian tradition comes down from generation to generation, each generation must hand it on uncorrupted and undistorted. There are times when that is difficult. The word Jude uses for *to defend* is *epagōnizesthai*, which contains the root of our English word *agony*. The defence of the faith may well be a costly thing; but that defence is a duty which falls on every generation of the Church.

THE PERIL FROM WITHIN

Jude 4

> For certain men have wormed their way into the Church
> – long before this, they were designated for judgment –
> impious creatures they are – who twist the grace of God
> into a justification of blatant immorality and who deny
> our only Master and Lord, Jesus Christ.

HERE is the peril which made Jude lay aside the treatise he was about to write and take up his pen to write this burning letter. The threat came *from within the Church*.

Certain people, as the Authorized Version has it, had *crept in unawares*. The Greek (*pareisduein*) is a very expressive word. It is used of the plausible and seductive words of someone who pleads their case cleverly, seeping gradually into the minds of a judge and jury; it is used of an outlaw slipping secretly back into the country from which he has been expelled; it is used of the slow and subtle entry of innovations into the life of society, which in the end undermine and break down the ancestral laws. It always indicates a stealthy insinuation of something evil into a society or situation.

Certain evil people had worked their way into the Church. They were the kind of people for whom judgment was waiting. They were irreverent and godless in their thoughts and in their lives. Jude picks out two characteristics about them.

(1) They perverted the grace of God into an excuse for blatant immorality. The Greek which we have translated as *blatant immorality* is a grim and terrible word (*aselgeia*). The corresponding adjective is *aselgēs*. Most people try to hide their sin; they have enough respect for common decency not to want to be found out. But those described as *aselgēs* are people who are so lost to decency that they do not care who sees their sin. It is not that they arrogantly and proudly flaunt it; it is simply that they can publicly do the most shameless things, because they have ceased to care for decency at all.

These people were undoubtedly tinged with Gnosticism and its belief that, since the grace of God was wide enough to cover any sin, they could sin as they liked. The more they sinned, the greater the grace – therefore, why worry about sin? Grace was being perverted into a justification for sin.

(2) They denied our only Lord and Master, Jesus Christ. There is more than one way in which people can deny Jesus Christ. (a) They can deny him in times of persecution. (b) They can deny him for the sake of convenience. (c) They can deny him by their lives and conduct. (d) They can deny him by developing false ideas about him.

If these people were Gnostics, they would have two mistaken ideas about Jesus. First, since the body, being matter, was evil, they would hold that Jesus only *seemed* to have a body and was a kind of spirit ghost in the apparent shape of a man. The Greek for *to seem* is *dokein*; and these people were called *Docetists*. They would deny the real humanity of Jesus Christ. Second, they would deny his uniqueness. They believed that there were many stages between the evil matter of this world and the perfect spirit which is God; and they believed that Jesus was only one of the many stages on the way.

No wonder Jude was alarmed. He was faced with a situation in which some had wormed their way into the Church, and these people were twisting the grace of God into a justification, and even a reason, for sinning in the most blatant way. They denied both the humanity and the uniqueness of Jesus Christ.

THE DREADFUL EXAMPLES

Jude 5–7

> It is my purpose to remind you – although you already possess full and final knowledge of all that matters – that, after the Lord had brought the people out of Egypt in safety, he subsequently destroyed those who were unbelieving; and that he has placed under guard in eternal chains in the abyss of darkness, to await the judgment which shall take place on the great day, the angels who did not keep their own rank but left their own proper habitation. Just so, Sodom and Gomorrah and the surrounding cities, who in the same way as these took their fill of sexual sin and strayed after perverted sexual immorality, are a warning by the way in which they paid the penalty of eternal fire.

1. THE FATE OF ISRAEL

JUDE issues a warning to the evil intruders who were perverting the belief and conduct of the Church. He tells them that he is, in fact, doing nothing other than reminding them of things of which they are perfectly well aware. In a sense, it is true to say that all preaching within the Christian Church is not so much bringing new truth as confronting people with truth they already know but have forgotten or are disregarding.

To understand the first two examples which Jude cites from history, we must understand one thing. The evil people who were corrupting the Church did not regard themselves as enemies of the Church and of Christianity; they regarded themselves as the advanced thinkers, a cut above the ordinary Christian, the spiritual elite. Jude chooses his examples to make clear that, even if people have received the greatest privileges, they may still fall away into disaster, and even those who have received the greatest privileges from God cannot consider themselves safe but must be on constant watch against mistaken beliefs and error.

The first example is from the history of Israel. He takes his story from Numbers 13–14. The mighty hand of God had delivered the people from slavery in Egypt. What greater act of deliverance could there be than that? The guidance of God had brought the people safely across the desert to the borders of the promised land. What greater demonstration of his providence could there be than that? So, at the very borders of the promised land, at Kadesh-barnea, spies were sent to spy out the land before the final invasion took place. With the exception of Caleb and Joshua, the spies came back with the opinion that the dangers ahead were so terrible, and the people so strong, that they could never win their way into the promised land. The people rejected the report of Caleb and Joshua, who were for going on, and accepted the report of those who insisted that the case was hopeless. This was a clear act of disobedience to God and of complete lack of faith in him. The consequence was that God gave sentence that of these people, with the exception of Joshua and Caleb, all those over the age of 20 would never enter the promised land but would wander in the wilderness until they were dead (Numbers 14:32–3, 32:10–13).

This was a picture which haunted the minds of both Paul and the writer to the Hebrews (1 Corinthians 10:5–11; Hebrews 3:18–4:2). It is the proof that even those who have the greatest privilege can meet with disaster before the end, if they fall away from obedience and lapse from faith. The Glasgow minister George Johnstone Jeffrey tells of a great man who absolutely refused to have his biography written before his death. 'I have seen', he said, 'too many men fall out on the last lap.' The Methodist John Wesley warned: 'Let, therefore, none presume on past mercies, as if they were out of danger.' In his dream, John Bunyan saw that even from the gates of heaven there was a way to hell.

Jude warns these intruders that, great as their privileges have been, they must still take care in case disaster should come upon them. It is a warning which each of us would do well to heed.

THE DREADFUL EXAMPLES

2. THE FATE OF THE ANGELS

Jude 5–7 (*contd*)

THE second dreadful example which Jude takes is the fallen angels.

The Jews had a very highly developed doctrine of angels, the servants of God. In particular, the Jews believed that every nation had its presiding angel. In the Septuagint, the Greek version of the Hebrew Scriptures, Deuteronomy 32:8 reads: 'When the Most High divided the nations, when he separated the sons of Adam, he set the bounds of the nations according to the number of the angels of God.' That is to say, to each nation there was an angel.

The Jews believed in a fall of the angels, and much is said about this in the Book of Enoch, which so often lies behind the thought of Jude. In regard to this, there were two lines of tradition.

(1) The first saw the fall of the angels as due to pride and rebelliousness. That legend gathered particularly round the name of Lucifer, the light-bringer, the son of the morning. As the Authorized Version has it, Isaiah writes: 'How art thou fallen from heaven, O Lucifer, son of the morning!' (Isaiah 14:12). When the Seventy returned from their mission and told Jesus of their successes, he warned them against pride: 'I watched Satan fall from heaven like a flash of lightning' (Luke 10:18). The idea was that there was civil war in heaven. The angels rose against God and were cast out; and Lucifer was the leader of the rebellion.

(2) The second stream of tradition finds its Scriptural echo in Genesis 6:1–4. In this line of thought, the angels, attracted by the beauty of mortal women, left heaven to seduce them and so sinned.

In the first case, the fall of the angels was due to *pride*; in the second case, it was due to *lust* for what was forbidden.

In effect, Jude takes the two ideas and puts them together. He says that the angels left their own rank; that is to say, they aimed at a position which was not for them. He also says that they left their own proper home; that is to say, they came to earth to live with mortal women.

All this seems strange to us; it moves in a world of thought and traditions from which we have moved away.

But Jude's warning is clear. Two things brought ruin to the angels – pride and lust. Even though they were angels, and heaven had been their dwelling place, they nonetheless sinned – and, for their sin, they were marked for judgment. To those reading Jude's words for the first time, the whole line of thought was plain, for Enoch had much to say about the fate of these fallen angels. So, Jude was speaking to his people in terms that they could well understand and was telling them that, if pride and lust ruined the angels in spite of all their privileges, pride and lust could ruin them as well. The evil intruders within the Church were proud enough to think that they knew better than the Church's teaching and were lustful enough to pervert the grace of God into a justification for blatant immorality. Whatever the ancient background of his words, Jude's warning is still valid. The pride which knows better than God and the desire for forbidden things are the way to ruin in time and in eternity.

THE DREADFUL EXAMPLES

3. SODOM AND GOMORRAH

Jude 5–7 (*contd*)

THE third example Jude chose is the destruction of Sodom and Gomorrah. Notorious for their sins, these cities were obliterated by the fire of God. The traveller and writer George Adam Smith, in *The Historical Geography of the Holy Land*, points out that no incident in history ever made such an impression on the Jewish people, and that Sodom and Gomorrah are time and time again used in Scripture as the supreme examples of human sin and the judgment of God; they are used in this way even by Jesus himself (Deuteronomy

29:23, 32:32; Amos 4:11; Isaiah 1:9, 3:9, 13:19; Jeremiah 23:14, 49:18, 50:40; Zephaniah 2:9; Lamentations 4:6; Ezekiel 16:46, 49, 53, 55; Matthew 10:15, 11:24; Luke 10:12, 17:29; Romans 9:29; 2 Peter 2:6; Revelation 11:8). 'The glare of Sodom and Gomorrah is flung down the whole length of Scripture history.'

The story of the final wickedness of Sodom and Gomorrah is told in Genesis 19:1-11, and the tragic tale of their destruction is told in the passage immediately following (Genesis 19:12-28). The sin of Sodom is one of the most horrible stories in history. H. E. Ryle, in his commentary on Genesis, has called it a 'repulsive incident'. The real horror of the incident is cloaked a little in the Authorized and Revised Versions by a Hebrew turn of speech. Two angelic visitors had come to Lot. He urged them to come in, and they entered his house as his guests. When they were there, the inhabitants of Sodom surrounded the house, demanding that Lot should bring out his visitors that they should *know* them. In Hebrew, *to know* is the word for sexual intercourse. It is said, for instance, that Adam *knew* his wife, and she conceived, and bore Cain (Genesis 4:1). What the men of Sodom were intent on was homosexual intercourse with Lot's two visitors – sodomy, the word in which their sin is commemorated.

It was after this that Sodom and Gomorrah were obliterated from the face of the earth. The neighbouring cities were Zoar, Admah and Zeboim (Deuteronomy 29:23; Hosea 11:8). This disaster was localized in the dreadful desert in the region of the Dead Sea, a region which George Adam Smith, who travelled extensively in Palestine, calls: 'This awful hollow, this bit of the infernal regions come to the surface, this hell with the sun shining into it.' It was there that the cities were said to have been; and it was said that under that scorched and barren earth there still smouldered an eternal fire of destruction. The soil is bituminous with oil below, and Adam Smith conjectures that what happened was this: 'In this bituminous soil took place one of these terrible explosions and conflagrations which have broken out in the similar geology of North America. In such soil reservoirs of oil and gas are formed, and suddenly discharged by their own pressure or by earthquake. The gas explodes, carrying high into the air masses of oil which fall back in fiery rain, and are so inextinguishable that they float afire on water.' It was by such an eruption of fire that Sodom and Gomorrah were destroyed. That awful desert was only a day's journey from Jerusalem, and this divine judgment on sin was never forgotten.

So, Jude reminds these evil people of the fate of those who in ancient times defied the moral law of God. Jude is insisting that they should remember that sin and judgment go hand in hand, and that they should repent in time.

CONTEMPT FOR THE ANGELS

Jude 8–9

> In the same way these, too, with their dreams, defile the flesh, and set at naught the celestial powers, and speak evil of the angelic glories. When the archangel Michael himself was disputing with the devil about the body of Moses, he did not venture to launch against him an evil-speaking accusation, but said: 'The Lord rebuke you!'

JUDE begins this passage by comparing the evil intruders with the false prophets whom Scripture condemns. Deuteronomy 13:1–5 sets down what is to be done with the person described in the Revised Standard Version as 'the prophet or the dreamer of dreams' who corrupts the nations and seduces the people from their loyalty to God. Such a prophet is to be mercilessly killed. These people whom Jude attacks are false prophets, dreamers of false dreams, seducers of the people, and must be treated as such. Their false teaching resulted in two things.

(1) It made them defile the flesh. We have already seen the twofold direction of their teaching on the flesh. First, the flesh was entirely evil, and, therefore, of no importance; and so the instincts of the body could be given their way without control. Second, the grace of God was all-forgiving and all-sufficient, and therefore sin did not matter since grace would forgive every sin. Sin was only the means whereby grace was given its opportunity to operate.

(2) They despised angels. Celestial powers and angelic glories are names for ranks of angels within the angelic hierarchy. This follows immediately after the citing of Sodom and Gomorrah as dreadful examples; and part of the sin of Sodom was the desire of its people to misuse its angelic visitors (Genesis 19:1–11). The people whom Jude attacks spoke evil of the angels. To prove how terrible a thing that was, Jude cites an instance from an apocryphal book, *The Assumption of Moses*. One of the strange things about Jude is that he so often makes his quotations from these apocryphal books. Such quotations seem strange to us; but these books were very widely used at the time when Jude was writing, and the quotations would be very effective.

The story in *The Assumption of Moses* runs as follows. The strange story of the death of Moses is told in Deuteronomy 34:1–6. *The Assumption of Moses* goes on to add the further story that the task of burying the body of Moses was given to the archangel Michael. The devil argued with Michael about possession of the body. He based his claim on two grounds. Moses' body was matter; matter was evil; and, therefore, the body belonged to him, for matter was his domain. Second, Moses was a murderer, for had he not slain the Egyptian whom he saw beating the Israelite (Exodus 2:11–12)? And, if he was a murderer, the devil had a claim on his body. The point Jude is making is this. Michael was engaged on a task given to him by God; the devil was seeking to stop him and was making claims he had no right to make. But, even in a chain of circumstances like that, Michael spoke no evil of the devil but simply said: 'The Lord rebuke you!' If the greatest of the good angels refused to speak evil of the greatest of the evil angels, even in circumstances like that, then surely no human being may speak evil of any angel.

What the people whom Jude is attacking were saying about the angels, we do not know. Perhaps they were saying that they did not exist; perhaps they were saying they were evil. This passage means very little to us, but no doubt it would be a weighty rebuke to those to whom Jude addressed it.

THE GOSPEL OF THE FLESH

Jude 10

> But these people speak evil of everything which they do not understand, whereas they allow themselves to be corrupted by the knowledge which their instincts give them, living at the mercy of their instincts, like beasts without reason.

JUDE says two things about the evil intruders whom he is attacking.

(1) They criticize everything which they do not understand. Anything which is out of their sphere of operation and their experience they disregard as worthless and irrelevant. 'Spiritual things are spiritually discerned' (cf. 1 Corinthians 2:14). They have no spiritual discernment, and, therefore, they are blind to, and contemptuous of, all spiritual realities.

(2) They allow themselves to be corrupted by the things they do understand. What they do understand are the sensual instincts which they share with animals. Their way of life is to allow these instincts to have their way; their values are values of the flesh. Jude is describing people who have lost all awareness of spiritual things and for whom the things demanded by their animal instincts are the only standards.

The terrible thing is that the first condition is the direct result of the second. The tragedy is that no one is born without a sense of the spiritual things; but it is possible to lose that sense so that spiritual things cease to exist. We may lose any faculty if we refuse to use it. We discover this in such simple things as games and skills. If we give up playing a game, we lose the ability to play it. If we give up practising a skill – such as playing the piano – we lose it. We discover this in such things as abilities. We may know something of a foreign language; but, if we never speak or read it, we lose it. We can all hear the voice of God; and we all have the animal instincts on which the future existence of the race depends. But, if we consistently refuse to listen to God and make our instincts the sole force behind our conduct, in the end we will be unable to hear the voice of God and will have nothing left to take control of us but basic desires. It is a terrible thing for people to reach a stage where they are deaf to God and blind to goodness; and that is the stage which the people whom Jude attacks had reached.

LESSONS FROM HISTORY

Jude 11

> Woe to them because they walk in the way of Cain;
> they fling themselves into the error of Balaam; they
> perish in Korah's opposition to God.

JUDE now goes to the history of Israel for parallels to the
wicked people of his own day; and from it he draws the
examples of three notorious sinners.

(1) First, there is Cain, the murderer of his brother Abel
(Genesis 4:1–15). In Hebrew tradition, Cain stood for two
things. (a) He was the first murderer in the world's history;
and, as the Wisdom of Solomon has it, 'he perished because
in rage he killed his brother' (Wisdom 10:3). It may well
be that Jude is implying that those who delude others are
nothing other than murderers of the souls of men and
women and are, therefore, the spiritual descendants of Cain.
(b) But, in Hebrew tradition, Cain came to stand for something
more than that. In the writings of Philo, he stands for
selfishness. In the Rabbinic teaching, he is the type of the
cynical man. In the Jerusalem *Targum*, he is depicted as
saying: 'There is neither judgment nor judge; there is no
other world; no good reward will be given to the good and
no vengeance taken on the wicked; nor is there any pity in
the creation or the government of the world.' To the Hebrew
thinkers, Cain was the cynical, materialistic unbeliever
who believed neither in God nor in the moral order of the
world and who, therefore, did exactly as he liked. So, Jude
is charging his opponents with defying God and denying
the moral order of the world. It remains true that those
who choose to sin still have to reckon with God and to
learn, always with pain and sometimes with tragedy, that no

one can defy the moral order of the world and escape the consequences.

(2) Second, there is Balaam. In Old Testament thought, in Jewish teaching and even in the New Testament (Revelation 2:14), Balaam is the great example of those who taught Israel to sin. In the Old Testament, there are two stories about him. One is quite clear, and very vivid and dramatic. The other is more obscure, but much more terrible; and it is this second story which left its mark on Hebrew thought and teaching.

The first is in Numbers 22–4. There, it is told how Balak attempted to persuade Balaam to curse the people of Israel, for he feared their power. Balaam was asked five times and offered large rewards. He refused to be persuaded by Balak; but his envy and greed stand out, and it is clear that only the fear of what God would do to him kept him from striking a dreadful bargain. Balaam already emerges from this story as a detestable character.

In Numbers 25, there is the second story. Israel is seduced into the worship of Baal with dreadful and repulsive moral consequences. As we read later (Numbers 31:8, 31:16), it was Balaam who was responsible for that seduction, and he perished miserably because he taught others to sin.

Out of this composite story, Balaam stands for two things. (a) He stands for the greedy and envious person who was prepared to sin in order to gain reward. (b) He stands for the evil person who was guilty of the greatest of all sins – that of teaching others to sin. So, Jude is accusing the wicked people of his own day that they are ready to leave the way of righteousness to make gain, and that they are teaching others to sin. To sin for the sake of gain is bad; but to teach another to sin is the worst sin of all.

(3) Third, there was Korah. His story is in Numbers 16:1–35. The sin of Korah was that he rebelled against the guidance

of Moses when the sons of Aaron and the tribe of Levi were made the priests of the nation. That was a decision which Korah was not willing to accept; he wanted to exercise a function which he had no right to exercise; and, when he did so, he perished terribly and all his companions in wicked-ness with him. Korah stands for those who refuse to accept authority and reach out for things which they have no right to have. So, Jude is charging his opponents with defying the legitimate authority of the Church and therefore preferring their own way to the way of God. We should remember that, if we take certain things which pride incites us to take, the consequences can be disastrous.

A PICTURE OF THE WICKED

Jude 12–16

These people are hidden rocks which threaten to wreck your Love Feasts. These are the people who at your feasts revel with their own cliques without a qualm. They have no feeling of responsibility to anyone except themselves. They are clouds which drop no water but are blown past by the wind. They are fruitless trees in autumn's harvest time, twice dead and torn up by the roots. They are wild sea waves, frothing out their own shameless deeds. They are wandering stars, and the abyss of darkness has been prepared for them forever. It was of these, too, that Enoch, who was the seventh from Adam, prophesied when he said: 'Behold, the Lord has come with ten thousands of his holy ones, to execute judgment upon all and to convict all the impious for all the deeds of their impiousness, which they have impiously committed, and for the harsh things which impious sinners have said against him.' For these people are grumblers. They querulously complain against the part in life which God has allotted to them. Their conduct is governed by their desires. Their mouths speak swelling words. They toady to men for what they can get out of it.

THIS is one of the great passages of invective of the New Testament. It is a blaze of moral indignation at its hottest. As James Moffatt puts it, 'Sky, land and sea are ransacked for illustrations of the character of these men.' Here is a series of vivid pictures, every one with significance. Let us take them one by one.

(1) They are like hidden rocks which threaten to wreck the Love Feasts of the Church. This is the one case in which there is doubt about what Jude is actually saying; but of one thing there is no doubt – the evil intruders were a danger to the Love Feasts. The Love Feast, the *Agape*, was one of the earliest features of the Church. It was a meal of fellowship held on the Lord's Day, and to it people brought what they could to be shared. It was a lovely idea that the Christians in each little house church should sit down on the Lord's Day to eat in fellowship together. No doubt, there were some who could bring much and others who could bring only little. For many of the slaves, it was perhaps the only decent meal they ever ate.

But very soon, the *Agape* began to go wrong. We can see it going wrong in the church at Corinth, when Paul declares that at the Corinthian Love Feasts there is nothing but division. They are divided into cliques and sections; some have too much, and others get nothing to eat; and the meal for some has become a drunken revel (1 Corinthians 11:17–22). Unless the *Agape* was a true fellowship, it was a travesty; and very soon it had begun to misrepresent its name completely.

Jude's opponents were making a travesty of the Love Feasts. The Revised Standard Version says that he calls them 'blemishes on your love feasts' (verse 12); and that agrees with the parallel passage in 2 Peter – 'blots and blemishes' (2 Peter 2:13). We have translated Jude's expression as 'hidden rocks'.

The difficulty is that Peter and Jude do not use the same word, although they use words which are very similar. The word in 2 Peter is *spilos*, which unquestionably means a *blot* or *spot*; but the word in Jude is *spilas*, which is very rare. Just possibly, it may mean a *blot*, because in later Greek it could be used for the spots and markings on an opal stone. But, in ordinary Greek, by far its most common meaning was *a submerged*, or *half-submerged*, *rock on which a ship could be easily wrecked*. We think that here the second meaning is much more likely.

In the Love Feast, people were very close together in heart, and there was the kiss of peace. These wicked people were using the Love Feasts as a cover for gratification of their lusts. It is a dreadful thing if people come into the Church and use the opportunities which its fellowship gives for their own ends. These people were like sunken rocks on which the fellowship of the Love Feasts was in danger of being wrecked.

THE SELFISHNESS OF THE WICKED

Jude 12–16 (*contd*)

(2) These wicked intruders revel in their own in-groups and have no feeling of responsibility for anyone except themselves. These two things go together, for they both stress the essential selfishness of these people.

(a) They revel in their own in-groups without a qualm. This is exactly the situation which Paul condemns in 1 Corinthians. The Love Feast was supposed to be an act of fellowship; and the fellowship was demonstrated by the sharing of all things. Instead of sharing, the wicked kept to their own group and kept to themselves all they had. In 1 Corinthians, Paul actually goes to the lengths of saying that the Love Feast could become a drunken revel in which people grabbed at everything they could get (1 Corinthians 11:21). People can never claim to know what church membership means if, in the Church, they are out for what they can get and they remain within their own little group.

(b) We have translated the next phrase as: 'They have no feeling of responsibility for anyone except themselves.' The Greek literally means 'shepherding themselves'. The duty of a leader of the Church is to be a shepherd of the flock of God (Acts 20:28). The false shepherd cared far more for himself than for the sheep which were supposed to be within his care. Ezekiel describes the false shepherds from whom their privileges were to be taken away: 'As I live, says the Lord God, because my sheep have become a prey, and my sheep have become food for all the wild animals, since there was no shepherd; and because my shepherds have not searched for my sheep, but the shepherds have fed themselves, and have not fed my sheep . . . I am against the shepherds; and I will demand my sheep at their hand, and put a stop to their feeding the sheep' (Ezekiel 34:8–10). Those who feel no responsibility for the welfare of anyone except themselves stand condemned.

So, Jude condemns the selfishness which destroys fellowship and the lack of any sense of responsibility for others.

(3) The wicked are like clouds blown past by the wind that drop no rain and like trees in harvest time that have no

fruit. These two phrases go together, for they describe people who make great claims but are essentially useless. There were times in Palestine when people would pray for rain. At such a time, a cloud might pass across the sky, bringing with it the promise of rain. But there were times when the promise was only an illusion, the cloud was blown on and the rain never came. In any harvest time, there were trees which looked as if they were heavy with fruit but which, when the time came to gather from them, gave no fruit at all.

At the heart of this lies a great truth. Promise without performance is useless, and in the New Testament nothing is so unsparingly condemned as uselessness. No amount of outward show or fine words will take the place of usefulness to others. As it has been put, 'If a man is not good for something, he is good for nothing.'

THE FATE OF DISOBEDIENCE

Jude 12–16 (*contd*)

JUDE goes on to use a vivid picture of these evil intruders. 'They are like wild sea waves frothing out their own shameless deeds.' The picture is this. After a storm, when the waves have been lashing the shore with their frothing spray and their foam, there is always left on the shore a fringe of seaweed and driftwood and all kinds of unsightly litter from the sea. That is always an unattractive scene. But in the case of one sea it is grimmer than in any other. The waters of the Dead Sea can be whipped up into waves, and these waves, too, cast up driftwood on the shore; but in this instance there is a unique circumstance. The waters of the Dead Sea are so impregnated with salt that they strip the bark from any driftwood in them; and, when such wood is cast up on the shore, it gleams bleak and white, more like dried bones than wood. The deeds of the wicked are like the useless and unsightly litter which the waves leave scattered on the beach after a storm and which resemble the skeleton-like relics of Dead Sea storms. The picture vividly portrays the ugliness of the deeds of Jude's opponents.

Jude uses yet another picture. The wicked are like the wandering stars that are kept in the depths of darkness for their disobedience. This is a picture taken directly from the Book of Enoch. In that book, the stars are sometimes identified with the angels; and there is a picture of the fate of the stars which, disobedient to God, left their appointed orbit and were destroyed. In his journey through the earth, Enoch came to a place where he saw 'neither the high heaven, nor the firmly founded earth, but a desert place, prepared and terrible'. He goes on: 'And there I saw seven stars of heaven bound on it together, like great mountains and burning like fire. Then I said, "For what sin have they been bound, and why have they been thrown here?" And Uriel, one of the holy angels who was with me and led me, spoke to me and said, "Enoch, about whom do you ask? About whom do you inquire and ask and care? These are some of the stars which transgressed the command of the Lord Most High, and they have been bound here until ten thousand ages are completed, the number of the days of their sin"' (1 Enoch 21:1–6). The fate of the wandering stars is typical of the fate of those who disobey God's commandments and, as it were, take their own way.

Jude then confirms all this with a prophecy; but the prophecy is again taken from Enoch. The actual passage runs: 'And behold! He comes with ten thousand holy ones to execute judgment upon them, and to destroy all the impious; and to contend with all flesh concerning everything which the sinners and the impious have done and wrought against him' (1 Enoch 1:9).

This quotation has raised many questions with regard to Jude and Enoch. There is no doubt that, in the days of Jude and in the days of Jesus, Enoch was a very popular book. Ordinarily, when the New Testament writers want to confirm their words, they do so with a quotation from the Old Testament, using it as the word of God. Are we then to regard Enoch as sacred Scripture, since Jude uses it exactly as he would have used one of the prophets? Or, are we to take the view of which Jerome speaks, and say that Jude cannot be Scripture, because it makes the mistake of using as Scripture a book which is, in fact, not Scripture?

We need waste no time on this debate. The fact is that Jude, a pious Jew, knew and loved the Book of Enoch and had grown up in a circle where it was regarded with respect and even reverence; and he takes his quotation from it perfectly naturally, knowing that his readers would recognize it and respect it. He is simply doing what all the New Testament writers do, as every writer must in every age, and speaking to men and women in language which they will recognize and understand.

THE CHARACTERISTICS OF THOSE WHO ARE EVIL

Jude 12–16 (*contd*)

IN verse 16, Jude sets down three last characteristics of the evil intruders.

(1) They are grumblers, always discontented with the life which God has allotted to them. In this picture, he uses two

words, one which was very familiar to his Jewish readers and one which was very familiar to his Greek readers.

(a) The first is *goggustēs*. (*Gg* in Greek is pronounced *ng*.) The word describes the discontented voices of the murmurers and is the same as is so often used in the Greek Old Testament for the *murmurings* of the children of Israel against Moses as he led them through the wilderness (Exodus 15:24, 17:3; Numbers 14:29). Its very sound describes the low mutter of resentful discontent which rose from the rebellious people. These wicked people in the time of Jude are the modern counterparts of the murmuring children of Israel in the desert, people full of sullen complaints against the guiding hand of God.

(b) The second is *mempsimoiros*. It is made up of two Greek words – *memphesthai*, which means *to blame*, and *moira*, which means *one's allotted fate or life*. A *mempsimoiros* was someone who was always grumbling about life in general. Theophrastus was the great master of the Greek character sketch, and he has a mocking study of the *mempsimoiros*, which is worth quoting in full:

> Querulousness is an undue complaining about one's lot; the querulous man will say to him that brings him a portion from his friend's table: 'You begrudged me your soup or your collops, or you would have asked me to dine with you in person.' When his mistress is kissing him, he says: 'I wonder whether you kiss me so warmly from your heart.' He is displeased with Zeus, not because he sends no rain, but because he has been so long about sending it. When he finds a purse in the street, it is: 'Ah! but I never found a treasure.' When he has bought a slave cheap with much importuning the seller, he cries: 'I wonder if my bargain's too cheap to be good.' When they bring him the good news that he

has a son born to him, then it is: 'If you add that I have lost half my fortune, you'll speak the truth.' Should this man win a suit-at-law by a unanimous verdict, he is sure to find fault with his speech-writer for omitting so many of the pleas. And if a subscription has been got up for him among his friends, and one of them says to him: 'You can cheer up now,' he will say: 'What? when I must repay each man his share, and be beholden to him into the bargain?'

Here, vividly drawn by Theophrastus' subtle pen, is the picture of a man who can find something to grumble about in any situation. He can find some fault with the best of bargains, the kindest of deeds, the most complete of successes, the richest of good fortune. 'There is great gain in godliness combined with contentment' (1 Timothy 6:6); but the evil people are chronically discontented with life and with the place in life that God has given to them. There are few people more unpopular than chronic grumblers; and anyone who has a tendency to complain in this way might do well to remember that such grumbling is in its own way an insult to God.

(2) Jude reiterates a point about these wicked people, which he has made again and again – their conduct is governed by their desires. To them, self-discipline and self-control are nothing; to them, the moral law is only a burden and a nuisance; honour and duty have no claim upon them; they have no desire to serve and no sense of responsibility. Their one value is pleasure, and their only motivating force is desire. If everyone was like that, the world would be in complete chaos.

(3) They speak with pride and arrogance, yet at the same time they are ready to pander to the great, if they think that they can get anything out of it. It is perfectly possible for them to talk themselves up in front of people they want

to impress and also to flatter and butter up those whom they think are important. Jude's opponents are glorifiers of themselves and flatterers of others, as they think the occasion demands; and their descendants are sometimes still among us.

THE CHARACTERISTICS OF ERROR (1)

Jude 17–19

> But you, beloved, you must remember the words which were once spoken by the apostles of our Lord Jesus Christ; you must remember that they said to us: 'In the last time there will be mockers, whose conduct is governed by their own impious desires.' These are the people who set up divisions – fleshly creatures, without the Spirit.

JUDE points out to his own people that nothing has happened which they might not have expected. The apostles had given warning that, in the last times, evil people would come, and such people are now among them. The actual words of Jude's quotation are not in any New Testament book. He may be doing any one of three things. He may be quoting from some apostolic book which we no longer possess. He may be quoting not a book but some oral tradition of the apostolic preaching, or some sermon which he himself had heard from the apostles. He may be giving the general sense of a passage like 1 Timothy 4:1–3. In any event, he is telling his people that error was only to be expected in the Church. From this passage, we can see some of the characteristics of these evil people.

(1) They mock at goodness, and their conduct is governed by their own evil desires. The two things go together. These

227

opponents of Jude had two characteristics, as we have already seen. They believed that the body, being matter, was evil; and that, therefore, it made no difference if they satisfied their desires to the full. Further, they argued that, since grace could forgive any sin, sin did not matter. These heretics had a third characteristic. They believed that they were the progressive thinkers; and they regarded those who observed the old moral standards as old-fashioned and out of date.

That point of view is by no means dead. There are still those who believe that the once-accepted standards of morality and fidelity, especially in matters of sex, are quite out of date. There is a terrible text in the Old Testament: 'Fools say in their hearts, "There is no God"' (Psalm 53:1). In that text, *fools* does not mean brainless individuals; it means people who are playing the fool. And the fact that they say there is no God is entirely due to wishful thinking. They know that, if there is a God, they are wrong and can expect judgment; therefore, they eliminate God. In the last analysis, those who eliminate the moral law and give free rein to their passions and desires do so because they want to do as they like. They listen to themselves instead of listening to God – and they forget that there will come a day when they will be compelled to listen to him.

THE CHARACTERISTICS OF ERROR (2)

Jude 17–19 (*contd*)

(2) These evil people have a second characteristic. They set up divisions – they are 'fleshly creatures, without the Spirit'. Here is a most significant thought – to set up divisions within the Church is always sin. These people set up divisions in two ways.

(a) As we have already seen, even at the Love Feasts they had their own little in-groups. By their conduct, they were steadily destroying fellowship within the Church. They were drawing a circle to shut people out instead of drawing a circle to take them in.

(b) But they went further. There were certain thinkers in the early Church who had a way of looking at human nature which essentially split people into two classes. To understand this, we must know something of Greek psychology. To the Greeks, human beings were made up of body (*sōma*), soul (*psuchē*) and spirit (*pneuma*). *Sōma* was simply a person's physical construction. *Psuchē* is more difficult to understand. To the Greeks, *soul*, *psuchē*, was simply *physical life*; everything that lived and breathed had *psuchē*. *Pneuma*, *spirit*, was quite different, it belonged only to human beings, and was the quality which made them thinking creatures, kin to God, able to speak to God and to hear him.

These thinkers went on to argue that everyone possessed *psuchē*, but very few really possessed *pneuma*. Only the really intellectual, the elite, possessed *pneuma*; and, therefore, only the very few could rise to real religion. The rest must be content to walk on the lower levels of religious experience.

They therefore divided people into two classes. There were the *psuchikoi*, who were physically alive but intellectually and spiritually dead. We might call them *the fleshly creatures*. All they possessed was flesh-and-blood life; intellectual progress and spiritual experience were beyond them. There were the *pneumatikoi*, who were capable of real intellectual knowledge, real knowledge of God and real spiritual experience. Here was the creation of an intellectual and spiritual aristocracy over against the common mass of people.

Further, these people who believed themselves to be the *pneumatikoi* believed that they were exempt from all the ordinary laws governing conduct. Ordinary people might have to observe the accepted standards; but they were above that. For them, sin did not exist; they were so advanced that they could do anything and be none the worse. We may do well to remember that there are still people who believe that they are above the laws, who say in their hearts that it could never happen to them and who believe that they can get away with anything.

We can now see how cleverly Jude deals with these people who say that the rest of the world are the *psuchikoi*, while they are the *pneumatikoi*. Jude takes their words and reverses them. 'It is you', he thunders at them, 'who are the *psuchikoi*, the flesh-dominated; it is you who possess no *pneuma*, no real knowledge and no experience of God.' Jude is saying to these people that, although they think of themselves as the only truly religious people, they have no real religion at all. Those whom they despise are, in fact, much better than they are themselves.

The truth about these so-called intellectual and spiritual people was that they wanted to sin and twisted religion into a justification for sin.

THE CHARACTERISTICS OF GOODNESS

Jude 20–1

> But you, beloved, must build yourselves up on the foundation of your most holy faith; you must pray in the Holy Spirit; you must keep yourselves in the love of God, while you wait for the mercy of our Lord Jesus Christ which will bring you to life eternal.

In the previous passage, Jude described the characteristics of error; here he describes the characteristics of goodness.

(1) Good people build up their lives on the foundation of the most holy faith. That is to say, the lives of Christians are founded not on something which they manufactured themselves, but on something which they received. There is a chain in the transmission of the faith. The faith came from Jesus to the apostles; it came from the apostles to the Church; and it comes from the Church to us.

There is something tremendous here. It means that the faith which we hold is not merely someone's personal opinion; it is a revelation which came from Jesus Christ and was preserved and transmitted within his Church, always under the care and the guidance of the Holy Spirit, from generation to generation.

That faith is a *most holy faith*. Again and again, we have seen the meaning of this word *holy*. Its root meaning is *different*. That which is *holy* is *different* from other things, as the priest is different from other worshippers, the Temple different from other buildings, the Sabbath different from other days and God supremely different from men and women.

Our faith is different in two ways. (a) It is different from other faiths and from philosophies in that it is not made by us but is God-given, not opinion but revelation, not guessing but certainty. (b) It is different in that it has the power to make those who believe it different. It is not only a mind-changer but also a life-changer, not only an intellectual belief but also a moral force.

(2) Good people are people who pray. It has been put this way: 'Real religion means *dependence*.' The essence of religion is the admission of our total dependence on God; and prayer is the acknowledging of that dependence, and the going to God for the help we need. As James Moffatt has it in a magnificent definition, 'Prayer is love in need

appealing to love in power.' Christians must be men and women of prayer for at least two reasons. (a) They know that they must test everything by the will of God and, therefore, they must take everything to God for his approval. (b) They know that of themselves they can do nothing, but that with God all things are possible and, therefore, they must always be taking their insufficiency to God's sufficiency.

Prayer, says Jude, is to be *in the Holy Spirit*. What he means is this. Our human prayers are at least sometimes bound to be selfish and blind. It is only when the Holy Spirit takes full possession of us that our desires are so purified that our prayers are right. The truth is that, as Christians, we are bound to pray to God; but he alone can teach us how to pray and what to pray for.

(3) Good people keep themselves in the love of God. What Jude is thinking of here is the old covenant relationship between God and his people as described in Exodus 24:1–8. God came to his people promising that he would be their God and they would be his people; but that relationship depended on their accepting and obeying the law which he gave them.

'God's love', Moffatt comments, 'has its own terms of communion.' It is true in one sense that we can never drift beyond God's love and care; but it is also true that, if we desire to remain in close communion with God, we must give him the perfect love and the perfect obedience which must always go hand in hand.

(4) Good people wait with expectation. They wait for the coming of Jesus Christ in mercy, love and power; for they know that Christ's purpose for them is to bring them to life eternal, which is nothing other than the life of God himself.

RECLAIMING THE LOST

Jude 22–3

> Some of them you must argue out of their error, while
> they are still wavering. Others you must rescue by
> snatching them out of the fire. Others you must pity
> and fear at the same time, hating the garment stained
> by the flesh.

DIFFERENT translators give differing translations of this
passage. The reason is that there is considerable doubt as to
what the true Greek text is. We have given the translation
which we believe to be nearest to the sense of the passage.

Even to the worst heretics, even to those most far gone in
error and to those whose beliefs are most dangerous, Christians
have a binding duty not to destroy but to save. Their aim must
be not to banish them from the Christian Church but to win
them back into the Christian fellowship. The theologian James
Denney of Glasgow Free Church College said that, to put the
matter at its simplest, Jesus came to make bad people good.
The historian Sir John Seeley said: 'When the power of
reclaiming the lost dies out of the church, it ceases to be the
church.' As we have taken this passage, Jude divides those
who cause trouble for the Church into three classes, to each
of whom a different approach is necessary.

(1) There are those who are flirting with falsehood. They
are obviously attracted by the wrong way and are on the brink
of committing themselves to error, but are still hesitating
before taking the final step. They must be argued out of their
error while there is time. From this, two things emerge as a
duty.

(a) We must study to be able to defend the faith and to
give a reason for the hope that is in us. We must know what
we believe so that we can meet error with truth; and we must

make ourselves able to defend the faith in such a way that our graciousness and sincerity may win others to it. To do this, we must banish all uncertainty from our minds and all arrogance and intolerance from our approach to others.

(b) We must be ready to speak in time. Many people would have been saved from error of thought and of action, if someone else had only spoken in time. Sometimes we hesitate to speak; but there are many times when silence is cowardly and can cause more harm than speaking out could ever cause. One of the greatest tragedies in life is when someone comes to us and says: 'I would never have been in the mess I am now in if someone – you, perhaps – had only spoken to me.'

(2) There are those who have to be snatched from the fire. They have actually started out on the wrong way and have to be stopped, as it were, forcibly, and even against their will. It is all very well to say that we must leave people their freedom and that they have a right to do what they like. All these things are in one sense true, but there are times when people must be – even forcibly – saved from themselves.

(3) There are those whom we must pity and fear at one and the same time. Here, Jude is thinking of something which is always true. There is danger to the sinner; but there is also danger to the rescuer. Anyone who aims to cure an infectious disease runs the risk of infection. Jude says that we must hate the garment stained by the flesh. Almost certainly, he is thinking here of the regulations in Leviticus 13:47–52, where it is laid down that the garment worn by a person discovered to be suffering from leprosy must be burned. The old saying remains true – we must love the sinner but hate the sin. Before we can rescue others, we must be strong in the faith ourselves. Our own feet must be firm on the dry land before we can throw a lifebelt to the person who is likely to be swept away.

The simple fact is that the rescue of those in error is not for everyone to attempt. Those who would win others for Christ must themselves be very sure of him; and those who would fight the disease of sin must themselves have the strong antiseptic of a healthy faith. Ignorance can never be met with ignorance, nor even with partial knowledge; it can be met only by the affirmation: 'I know whom I have believed.'

THE FINAL ASCRIPTION OF PRAISE

Jude 24–5

> Unto him who is able to keep you from slipping and to make you stand blameless and exultant in the presence of his glory, to the only God, our Saviour, through Jesus Christ our Lord, be glory, majesty, dominion and power, before all time, at this present time, and for all time. Amen.

JUDE comes to an end with a tremendous ascription of praise.

Three times in the New Testament, praise is given to *the God who is able*. In Romans 16:25, Paul gives praise to the God who is able to strengthen us. God is the one person who can give us a foundation for life which nothing and no one can ever shake. In Ephesians 3:20, Paul gives praise to the God who is able to do far more than we can ever ask or even dream of. He is the God whose grace no one has ever exhausted and on whom no claim can ever be too much.

Here, Jude offers *his* praise to the God who is able.

(1) God is able to keep us from slipping. The word is *aptaistos*. It is used both of a sure-footed horse which does not stumble and of a person who does not fall into error. 'He will not let your foot be moved' – or, as the Scottish metrical version has it, 'Thy foot he'll not let

slide' (Psalm 121:3). To walk with God is to walk in safety even on the most dangerous and the most slippery path. In mountaineering, climbers are roped together so that, even if the inexperienced climber should slip, the skilled mountaineer can take the weight and save the other person. In the same way, when we bind ourselves to God, he keeps us safe.

(2) He can make us stand blameless in the presence of his glory. The word for *blameless* is *amōmos*. This is characteristically a sacrificial word; and it is commonly and technically used of an animal which is without spot or blemish and is therefore fit to be offered to God. The amazing thing is that, when we submit ourselves to God, his grace can make our lives nothing less than a sacrifice fit to offer to him.

(3) He can bring us into his presence exultant. Surely the natural way to think of entry into the presence of God is in fear and in shame. But, by the work of Jesus Christ and in the grace of God, we know that we can go to God with joy and with all fear banished. Through Jesus Christ, God the stern Judge has become known to us as God the loving Father.

We note one last thing. Usually we associate the word *Saviour* with Jesus Christ; but here Jude attaches it to God. He is not alone in this, for God is often called Saviour in the New Testament (Luke 1:47; 1 Timothy 1:1, 2:3, 4:10; Titus 1:3, 2:10, 3:4). So, we end with the great and comforting certainty that at the back of everything there is a God whose name is Saviour. Christians have the joyous certainty that in this world they live in the love of God and that in the next world they go to that love. The love of God is both the atmosphere and the goal of all their living.